Phil Boast was formerly a landscape g[illegible]. Paula Larcher was an HR Director for the Civil Service. The couple met in Surrey, and travelled extensively in South East Asia before moving to North Sulawesi, Indonesia

BAHOWO LODGE

An Indonesian Affair

Phil Boast and Paula Larcher

Book Guild Publishing

Sussex, England

First published in Great Britain in 2011 by
The Book Guild Ltd
19 New Road
Brighton, BN1 1UF

Typeset in Baskerville by Ellipsis Books Limited, Glasgow

Printed in Great Britain by
CPI Antony Rowe

A catalogue record for this book is available from The British Library.

ISBN 978 1 84624 607 4

Contents

Foreword

The following is a story, or perhaps we should say a history, since all of the events that are recounted hereafter happened as they are written, without exaggeration or embellishment, and all of the people referred to are real and very much alive, and mostly still a part of our lives.

It is the account of how two English people in their forties found themselves living in a quiet fishing village called Bahowo, in North Sulawesi, Indonesia, and how they came to build and run a small hotel, which is called Bahowo Lodge.

And we are still here, living in this tranquil backwater of the world, offering food, shelter and, we hope, sharing our experiences with travellers from around the world, who come here to dive the magnificent coral reefs of Bunaken National Marine Park, or in search of the unique and beautiful flora and fauna of North Sulawesi. Or maybe some are just on a voyage of discovery, as we were when we first came.

The following narrative, then, is an attempt to write down in words the journey that brought us here, from the leafy suburbs of Surrey where we grew up, and thence from Sussex and London where we made our English homes.

Aside from any motivations of our own to recount our

experiences, the book is largely the result of evenings spent at the lodge with guests and friends, when, usually over the evening meal, we would recount tales and episodes of our journey here and events that have occurred since we arrived. Many times we have been told that we should 'write a book about it', and we have oft times considered doing so, despite perhaps being somewhat daunted by the prospect. The final 'spark' that ignited our launch into the literary world occurred in an unguarded moment one evening as we were, as it happens, alone and celebrating Paula's birthday with a few glasses of wine. In such situations one's inhibitions and reservations can be overcome; we agreed that we should attempt the book, touched glasses on it, and from that moment there was no going back. The next morning, despite feeling somewhat the worse for wear, I sat in front of a blank computer screen with a large mug of strong black coffee, and began to write this book.

It is not a story intended to change lives (although, you never know), or to make definitive comment upon matters of great importance, but is rather a personal account of the last ten or so years of our lives. If there is an underlying philosophy to the way we lived these years, then this will perhaps become clear during the pages of this book, and who knows, perhaps it will become clearer to us for the writing down.

For now we will concern ourselves with imparting the events as they happened, and as we saw them. The first chapters of the book are an account of our eventual arrival in Bahowo, and some of the circumstances and thoughts that led us here, and of the building of Bahowo Lodge. This is recounted more or less in chronological order. In subsequent chapters we have attempted to pull together certain aspects of our lives after our arrival in Indonesia; the people, their customs, and the everyday occurrences that have shaped their lives and ours. In the later chapters we bring the story back to ourselves once more, and attempt to make some sense of our time in Bahowo to date, and of our lives as they are now. Whether we have succeeded in so doing, we can, in the end, only leave to your judgement.

1

About the Authors

Before we commence our narrative, may we briefly introduce ourselves, in order that you may, if you wish, put us and our story into some kind of context. Those not particularly interested may skip this chapter, as it has no direct bearing upon or relevance to the story that follows hereafter.

Paula was born of half English and half Irish parentage, it being her grandfather, 'Papa', who made the family money. She is the academic brains behind the operation, and attended Woking Grammar School for Girls, being in the fifth form of this fine institution when we met. At that time I was working as a gardener for Guildford Parks Department, having left school in the lower sixth. Paula went on to do her first degree in sociology at The University of Sussex, and subsequently, some years later, a masters degree in employment law from Leicester, picking up a further degree in human resources along the way. She became a civil servant on leaving university and rose swiftly through the ranks until eventually becoming head of her own human resources department; she was in charge of in the region of six hundred and fifty staff by the time we put a premature end to our respective careers in England and moved, as this story is about to tell, to Indonesia.

I was born of English parents, somewhat on the other side of the tracks, attended probably the worst school in Surrey (and one would imagine a fair way beyond its borders) and at the age of sixteen decided that such an education is all very well but there must be more to it than this. I thought that the great outdoors, and gardens in particular, would be a good place in which to work, and so, having secured a job with the aforementioned parks department for a year, went on to continue my education at Merrist Wood Agricultural College near Guildford, taking a three-year course in landscape gardening. From thence I set up in business, initially in a small way with a pick-up truck and some tools, and spent the next two decades and more landscaping the gardens of Sussex and beyond, the highest accolade from this time being the construction of a couple of gold-medal-winning gardens at the Chelsea Flower Show.

Any associations with or similarities between our early relationship and *Lady Chatterley's Lover* may not be entirely without foundation. Being a gardener can have its advantages against the backdrop of such fine literature.

We misspent the early part of our youth mainly in Guildford, where we met and fell instantly in love. Our romance began, for anybody familiar with the town, in The Star public house in Quarry Street, which was at that time rather the place to be, although regretfully it has since, in common with so many such fine establishments, become homogenized, and has lost its soul. To revisit it now is to walk into an empty place, although if we listen hard enough we can still hear the laughter of our young, intense years echoing from the walls. By the time we met, Paula was sweet sixteen and I had just celebrated my seventeenth birthday. Once Paula had finished school, we rented a basement and then eventually bought our first flat in Brighton when Paula started university, and stayed on in this fine and vibrant city to buy a town house, an excellent venue for parties as many of our friends at the time will testify.

We eventually moved out of town and entered into our cottage phase, buying early seventeenth-century properties first in Upper Beeding, West Sussex, then in Ninfield, East Sussex, and eventually Yapton, West Sussex, where we still have our cottage. Concurrently with Brighton and Upper Beeding, we also bought and eventually sold a flat in Clapham, South London. (For those familiar with the area, it was up the dodgy end, within a stone's throw of Clapham North tube station.) We never married (never marry your lover) and as neither of us had any inclination to introduce a third party into the affair we never wanted or had children.

In the writing of this book, I have been the scribe, with Paula providing the detail, corrections, additions and always the inspiration. The book was written over the period of about two months, mostly between the hours of 4 and 6 a.m., when the world is quiet and dark, and before our guests awake to their day's activities. Paula would edit in the cold, or rather, warm light of day.

And so, our story begins. Where it will end for us we know not, but we can, at least, begin at the beginning.

2

Discovering Sulawesi

It was, as is probably often the case in such matters, part accident and part design that found us living in Bahowo village in the year of 2003.

The roots of the matter go back to our many holidays spent in South East Asia, and especially Borneo, where we travelled extensively together during holidays in our former lives, and where we left a part of our collective soul. We would hire a small canoe and local boatmen and travel along rivers as far into the interior as time would allow, being guests at night of the Dayaks who live there in long-houses, and in perfect harmony with the rainforest, their way of life having not changed for countless generations. These people were formerly head-hunters, whose fascinating culture is deserving of a book in its own right, and our times with them have left us a lasting legacy. On one such visit, I was presented with a blowpipe of some seven feet in length, having displayed a certain skill with its use; it remains amongst our most treasured possessions. We were also given some darts, and our generous hosts could not understand why we did not also take the poison necessary for applying to the tips before killing monkeys and so on. We told them that we had our own special English poison (required to kill special English monkeys), and they accepted this. Borneo in a sense became our second home, and we knew then that the rainforests would never thereafter give us peace and that we would one day try to make our home in the heat and wetness of the tropics.

So it was that one cold, wet evening in Sussex as we were habitually and casually browsing the atlas, the island of Sulawesi caught our attention. We had considered going there before, when on holiday in Bali, but the Balinese people had warned us not to go; the people, they said, were unfriendly and the island in general not a good place for tourists. We now know that the people of every Indonesian island say the same about every other Indonesian island, but in any case Sulawesi seemed to hold a certain fascination for us, and we were resolved to go there. It was, after all, just a short jump across the Wallace Line from our beloved Borneo, and it looked as though there should be some good diving and trekking there. Very few people we knew had ever heard of the place and, when asked, assumed that it was somewhere in Africa. This is perhaps understandable; after all, the name does sound rather African, and until the 1940s, and the end of Dutch colonial rule, it had been known as the Celebes Islands. Our travel agent at the time, who specialized in Asia, could offer us no guidance. She had never been there, but after some research and in the end by first going there herself, she contrived to organize for us a tour of the north peninsula. We gave ourselves a month to explore as much as possible and to do some jungle trekking and scuba diving.

Little need be said in this book of the trip itself, which was in September 2000, save that it gave us our first insight into our eventual home, and began our love affair with the island, its people and landscapes. North Sulawesi, being a narrow peninsula, has a rich and varied coastline with beautiful deserted sandy beaches, interspersed with mangrove forests and occasional coastal settlements. Travel away from the ocean and one finds oneself surrounded by spectacular volcanic highland scenery, cooler climates, fertile volcanic soil, sulphur lakes, padi fields and everywhere verdant green forests and the aroma of cloves. The people of North Sulawesi are always very friendly and greet you with a ready smile. In fact, North Sulawesi is known as the Land of the Smiling People and it is an apt description. Having hired a local guide and driver, we drove from the northern tip of the peninsula as far west as the Dumoga Bone National Park, which was in itself something of an achievement given the generally parlous state of the highways and byways of Sulawesi. Our journeys took us through various villages, each of which specialized in a certain type of fruit or spice, in each case symbolized by a concrete representation of their particular specialty at the centre of the village. For example, the pineapple village would have a huge concrete pineapple, the peanut village a huge peanut, and so on.

The eastern part of the peninsula of North Sulawesi is roughly divided into two districts. The district of Manado comprises most of the northern coastline and the outlying islands, and within its bounds lies the regional capital city of Manado. The district of Minahasa consists mainly of the highland areas, including the local volcanoes, and the southern coast, but also encompasses the extreme north-easterly tip of the peninsula. The capital of the Minahasa district is the town of Tomohon, known locally as the City of Flowers, since it is in this area that most of the local horticulture takes place. The flower markets of Tomohon are superb and offer a huge variety of plants and flowers, ranging from the more tropical types which one would expect, such as tropical hibiscus, gardenia and bougainvillea, to species normally associated with cooler climes, such as roses and hydrangeas. These latter types in fact only do well in the highlands, and our subsequent attempts to establish them in our warmer coastal location have been mostly unsuccessful. Nevertheless, as one travels around in this region one is struck by the amount and variety of colour, and the people's love of their gardens and all things that grow, flower and fruit. Plants such as dieffenbachia, grown in pots on the windowsill in England, grow wild by the roadside, and whilst on matters horticultural, one should also mention the wide range of spices grown here, which include nutmeg, ginger in many forms, turmeric, vanilla, lemongrass (which grows like a weed) and of course cloves and cinnamon, or sweet wood as it is known locally.

We spent some of our time exploring the highland areas of Minahasa, and it was here that we met an Indonesian lady who had spent many years of her life in Europe, but had now returned to live in this part of Indonesia. We spent a few evenings in her company, and during the course of our conversations we talked about the beautiful upland forests of the local Minahasa highlands and the people who live there. The whole area has an abundance of coconuts and dramatic flame trees, interspersed with huge bamboo and banana trees, which makes this such a lush and verdant landscape. All of this is set against a backdrop of spectacular volcanic scenery with a ridge of active volcanoes, vividly turquoise sulphur lakes and bubbling hot water springs. She told us that in her opinion the only thing lacking in the area was financial investment, particularly from abroad, and we discussed the possibility and practicality of foreigners buying land in Sulawesi. Although we have not seen her since, these conversations were, in an indirect sense, to become definitive in terms of our later plans, and helped to sow the seeds of our eventually living here.

During the tour we caused our guide much consternation by often changing our schedule at the last moment, a factor necessitated by the fact that we had no idea how long we should allow in the various places in order to see that which we came to see.

An example of this was our quest to seek out the unique and peculiar Maleo bird, which is endemic to Sulawesi. This bird, which is about the size of a chicken, has evolved to lay one huge egg weighing about one quarter of its own body weight. It buries the egg in the warm volcanic sands of the forest, then walks away to allow it to incubate itself, and the chick, once hatched, to dig its way back up to freedom and fresh air. Being seasoned jungle-trekkers, we allowed a couple of days of deep jungle work for the possibility of spotting such a rare bird (I should add that neither of us are bird-watchers, but we reckoned this one had to be seen), and to this end we pulled up in the general area of forest where Maleo birds are known to reside. They were everywhere. We could have got some good shots from the car and moved swiftly on, but decided that since we were there we may as well walk about a bit, knowingly spotting areas of warm sand where a Maleo bird might well bury its egg, if it were of a mind so to do.

Thus satisfied with our efforts, we paid in any case for our two nights' accommodation, which we had booked in advance, and drove onwards to further adventures, assuring our tour guide that he would not lose his job for deviating from the 'programme', and that the key aspect of such tours for Western people is flexibility. Each such deviation would require a prolonged and increasingly frantic phone conversation between our guide and HQ, to make sure that 'the boss' would know that it was the English, not he, who had changed the schedule. On eventually returning to HQ we received a knowing pep talk from 'the boss' about how he had always found that the important thing about tours involving Western people was flexibility. Thus it was that a new word was introduced into the jargon of North Sulawesi tourist organizations.

In telling this story it is our policy to use the real names of people wherever possible; however, we hope you will forgive us if we make two exceptions, for reasons that will become apparent as our story unfolds. Our tour guide we will therefore call Mr A. Despite later events, it was he who provided us with our next stepping stone to our new life, by offering his services as our 'friend' in Indonesia, should we wish to buy land, build a house or set up business here. Only later were we to learn and understand the importance of having 'friends' in Indonesia, and of choosing them carefully. At some point we must have said that we thought that something of this sort would be a good idea, and in any event agreed that we would perhaps return to Sulawesi some months hence. He in turn said that he would be willing, if we decided to come back, to research areas of land that were available for purchase.

And so it was that the events and ideas that were soon to become the dominant factors in our lives started with chance meetings and casual conversations. There was no moment of inspiration, clarity or certainty, but Sulawesi had begun to work its magic.

The idea and actuality of returning to England had become increasingly hard for us during our years of taking holidays in our beloved South East Asia. Nevertheless, we said our goodbyes and headed for home, stopping off for a couple of nights in Singapore on the way. It was here, over a few beers in a café on Clarke Quay, that we agreed and were resolved to take our first step into the unknown, and to return in due course to see what could be made of it all. After a few more beers we phoned Mr A and told him to go ahead and look for suitable land in the Minahasa highlands.

3

Back in England

Our resolve did not lessen when we returned to our working lives in England. It could, after all, have been a holiday aberration, inspired by the heat and romance of the moment, but we checked with ourselves and each other, and were both equally sure that this (whatever 'this' was) was what we wanted to do. We were not, it should be said, unhappy with our lot; in fact, our cup rather ranneth over, if you knoweth what I mean. Paula was in mid-flow, as it were, of a successful career, and was well set on the road to higher office, and the landscape gardening business was doing okay, despite being more sensitive to the vagaries of boom and recession that seemed to be the order of the day. On the whole we enjoyed our respective work, loved our cottage, and life was good. Nor was this some last-ditch attempt to salvage a dying relationship, as is sometimes the case it seems with these things, for we were as sure of our love for each other as ever, something that was to prove essential in later stages of our move to Indonesia.

We had always worked and played hard, and had perhaps arrived at a stage in life where, in certain respects, there was nowhere much better that we could be within the structure of our lives as they then were. Our house was big enough (in fact, as we would at times discuss, it was far bigger than we needed), neither of us were in the least interested in buying bigger or faster cars, the perfect sound system, designer kitchenware and so forth, and in all material senses we had all that we wished for, life was comfortable, and we had in a sense come to the end of our respective and mutual ambitions. We had reached a point where we needed a new challenge, and of course, shared a burning wish to live in South East Asia.

Having thus decided to continue with our venture, it seemed logical to us that our next port of call on returning to England should be the Indonesian Embassy in London, at least to see what useful information and help could be gleaned there in regard to living or setting up business in Indonesia. Anybody who has ever tried to telephone the Indonesian Embassy in London will know that this is a complete waste of time; all you ever get, it seems, is an answering machine, or at least this was our experience. Undaunted, we presented ourselves in person one afternoon, and were met by two very smart and charming Indonesian officials. Over tea and cakes, we told them broadly of our intention to move and perhaps set up business in Indonesia, and asked if they could help us. 'Yes, we can help you, please fill in this form.' We met several other officials during the course of the afternoon, and left with a fistful of business cards, none of which in the event proved to be any use whatsoever, and although nobody that we met had ever been to Sulawesi, everybody in our inexperienced eyes seemed helpful enough. What we know now, but did not know at the time, is that when dealing with Indonesian bureaucracy time goes into a strange warp, and hours can be spent in seemingly endless and circular discussion and more form-filling ('Please fill in this other form') and one is never quite sure what one has achieved at the end of it. It put one in mind rather of being in an episode of the *Twilight Zone*, for those familiar with the series, or maybe a Stephen King novel, where we had entered a place where the normal processes of logic and cause and effect go slightly off beam.

Nevertheless, when we finally emerged once more into the blinding and reassuring daylight of the London streets, feeling as though we had just undergone some mental or psychological ordeal, we did at least have an assurance that, on the basis of the forms that we had filled in, they would contact us with advice as to the best way to proceed. In fact, nothing happened. Not one letter, fax, email or telephone call resulted, and we began to think that we had perhaps imagined the whole event, or had suffered some kind of reverse collective amnesia and remembered something that had not actually happened. We now know, in the light of several years of finding ourselves in discussion with the many and varied offices of Indonesian government, that in such situations, in order to gain any momentum we would need to have gone back at least twice more and had the same discussions all over again. 'Please fill in this form.' It must be reassuring for any Indonesian citizens living in Britain that in one of the most modern, efficient, vibrant cities on the planet, there is a place that is forever Indonesia.

So we were on our own, and had to proceed as best we could. Let us return to the subject of buying land.

4

Bahowo

Geographically, the eastern end of peninsula North Sulawesi can be broadly divided into two regions; the 'Minahasa' highlands and upland areas, which consist of extinct, dormant and active volcanoes, and the lowland or coastal areas. The volcanoes are in fact a part of the much longer chain of volcanoes that extends to the north and south of Sulawesi, known as the 'ring of fire'. The highlands are cooler with much higher rainfall, and the people differ considerably between the two regions, ethnically and culturally. The original settlers were the highland people, who back in the mists of time lived out their stone-age lives around Lake Tondano, as it is now known, and whose descendants came to form the nine tribes of Minahasa. These have since rather melted together, largely since the coming of Christianity into the area, into one ethnic group known collectively as the Minahasa people, although they still retain some of their distinctive tribal customs. They have in general much finer features than the coastal people, and paler skin, and Minahasan women are generally thought of as being the most beautiful in Indonesia. They traditionally have a diet of rice, vegetables and anything that walks or crawls upon the earth, including snakes, bats, rats, dogs (the latter being somewhat

15

unpalatable to the sensibilities of dog-loving English people such as ourselves) and general forest animals. The symbol of the bringing together of the nine tribes of Minahasa is called Manguni, and he is an owl. Before any collective ceremony can begin, Manguni the owl must hoot nine times to symbolize each of the respective tribes.

The coastal people arrived much later from the Talaud-Sangihe Islands, which lie between Sulawesi and the Philippines, and from whence they brought their own distinctive culture. They settled along the northern coasts and local islands of Peninsula North Sulawesi, where they formed fishing and farming communities. Their diet is mainly yams, rice, fish and vegetables, and they find the eating of forest animals distasteful.

Culinary matters notwithstanding, we thought that the cooler highland climate would suit our northern European constitutions better, and it was this fact, aside from the stunning natural beauty of the place, that had made us decide that we would like to live in the highlands.

Thus it was that four months or so after our first visit here in 2000, we found ourselves once more back in Sulawesi and driving around Minahasa in search of prime and suitable real estate. By now it was January 2001 and the rainy season had set in, but as we have discovered since living here the distinction between the wet and dry seasons in North Sulawesi is largely academic, and we can get nearly as much rain in the 'dry' season as at any other time of year. Conversely, we can enjoy long periods of gloriously sunny weather during what are considered be the rainy months. Mr A had found us some beautiful locations, mostly on the sides of the volcanoes, where, due to the tropical sunshine, high rainfall and incredibly rich and fertile volcanic soil, much of the area is put over to vegetable, fruit and spice production. It still strikes us as an odd thing that since the generally cooler temperatures in the highlands allow for the growing of potatoes, carrots, cabbages and so on, the wares of market places in North Sulawesi resemble what one might find in an English market, only with the addition of various local vegetables, herbs, spices, exotic fruits and about ten different types of chilli.

The sites that Mr A showed us on our first day were beautiful, but despite not having any fixed ideas about where we would live, none of them were really working for us. There were few buildings or settlements to give us any kind of focus, so it was really all about location and views, as well as practical matters such as decent access roads, a local electricity supply and the availability of groundwater. In any event, we both agreed that for various reasons none of the locations were quite what we were looking for. In retrospect, the reason for this general feeling of dissatisfaction is blindingly obvious, but at the time we were not aware of it, at least consciously. For despite the loveliness of the place and the relatively cool climate, what was missing was the sea. The ocean was calling us, and we had to answer.

The next day we left the highlands and headed to the north coast. The coasts of North Sulawesi are largely deserted, the few fishing villages interspersed with long stretches of pristine, rocky or sandy coastline. Here we looked at locations that would have been well suited for a Robinson Crusoe film-set, a bit like Death Valley on Sea with palm trees. Certainly no tourists would ever have ventured here. Very beautiful it was, but, we decided, rather impractical as a place to settle, again given the absence of an electricity supply, the generally parlous state of the local roads, which would have made access for building materials difficult, the isolated location and probable absence of fresh water (you never know where the fresh water is in Sulawesi until you start digging).

Mr A was by now despairing of finding us a place that we would consider buying, and at the end of the third day of searching informed us that there was just one more place that he had found, in a small, quiet and isolated coastal village called Bahowo, but we would definitely not like it, the plot of land being as it was in a village location. We decided that we may as well look at it anyway and found Bahowo to be a traditional fishing village of small, predominantly bamboo and wooden houses with palm roofs, with its own black sand beach, upon which were moored the brightly coloured traditional fishing boats which are known locally as *londes* – basically a hollowed out log with bamboo stabilisers on each side. This being a totally Christian village there were two churches, one traditional Protestant and the other Pentecostal, and one small and dilapidated primary school. The village was surrounded on three sides by forest and coconut plantations. On the fourth side was the Sulawesi Sea, which lay beyond the fringing coral reef and mangrove forests. The village was and remains almost invisible from the main road (which is in truth little more than a track itself), and from the sea. Only by navigating through the mangrove forests can one approach Bahowo beach, and other than the church spire and nowadays Bahowo Lodge itself, which forms a landmark from the sea, there is nothing to indicate that any kind of settlement exists. The plot of land itself was essentially an area of scrubby jungle with a few coconut and banana trees at the far end of the village, next to the ocean but with no adjacent beach. The sea, however, lapped against its boundary at high tide and it had commanding views of the local group of islands. We had been there less than fifteen minutes before we knew without words that this was the right place.

Thus it was that we found Bahowo, and although throughout our venture our ideas had hitherto in a way built upon themselves, and would continue to do so, and events tended to create their own momentum, if one is looking for a defining moment when we decided that this would, if possible, be our new life, that moment would probably be it.

Aside from the fact that it immediately 'felt' right for both of us, Bahowo seemed, on first impression, to have several advantages. The location was quiet and relatively isolated, but it was only about 15 kilometres from the city of Manado, which is the regional capital. The village had a working beach, from which the small village fishing boats could pass through the mangrove forest and over the very shallow reef head. There was abundant fresh water, there being already one well close to the plot (we later built others, the digging of which we will recount in a following chapter), and the village had had an electricity supply for some eight years. We also, in fact, liked the idea of being part of a village community and our initial impressions and reception that we received from the people were all very positive. Indonesians, or certainly those that we have met, are for the most part friendly, warm individuals, with a ready smile and accommodating manner, and from our very first meeting we were made to feel welcome in Bahowo. Perhaps equally importantly, at least from a commercial point of view, there was a dive centre within a 10-minute drive, and so we formed the idea of setting up a lodge for scuba divers. Aside from these practical considerations, the land was and still is in a stunning location. We had the sea to the front, the mountains to our backs, and everything else was forest. From the balconies of what has since become Bahowo Lodge we can see no other human habitation, and the sea breezes can cool the warmest of tropical nights.

You will perhaps have noted that hitherto in our story, even if we eventually succeeded in making a new life for ourselves, whether it be in Sulawesi, Sarawak (the northern part of Borneo where we had spent many previous holidays) or elsewhere, we previously had had no clear idea what we would actually do once we got there. During our years of soul-searching in England, we had considered setting up a turtle hatchery (we know nothing about turtles), a palm plantation (we know less about palm trees) and other even more outlandish ideas that were mooted at various times. Indeed, one of the more difficult conundrums that we faced was how to pull together the careers of two people, one of whom is an employment law expert and the other a landscape gardener. It seemed that the only option for us was to do something that neither of us had the least idea how to do, and setting up a tourist lodge fitted comfortably into this category.

What we did have in our favour was the fact that, having travelled extensively in Asia and many other places besides, and stayed in five-star hotels, bamboo huts and everything in between, we knew the kind of place that we would like to stay in ourselves, and knew the things that we liked and disliked about holiday accommodation. We preferred somewhere small in terms of the number of guest rooms, personal and clean, with an informal 'homely' atmosphere. Our ideal would be to have such modern conveniences as air conditioning, and hot and cold showers, but not so far detached from local culture and people that one could effectively be anywhere in the world. Thus far on our travels around Sulawesi and elsewhere we had not found anywhere that fitted all of these criteria, and so we resolved, if it were to prove possible, to build it ourselves. We were by now perhaps beginning to get some focus on how we would proceed, and at least knew where we eventually wished to be. But first we had to buy the land.

So it was that we were first introduced to 'Mr Aris'. Aris is in fact his first name; however, it is a mark of respect hereabouts when addressing strangers, or in a formal situation, to prefix any name with 'Mr', or 'Pak' as it is in Indonesian. In the case of women, it is always 'Miss', whether the lady in question is married or not. In any case, Aris owned our newly found land, by virtue of the fact that he had inherited it from his forebears, and thus did we begin our friendship with him. He in fact eventually became our driver. We also, on our first and subsequent visits to the village, met Mr Benjamin, the village headman, who was to become a very important figure, particularly in later episodes of our venture, and various others of the village elders. Before we could even consider buying or building on Bahowo land, we would have to gain the agreement of the villagers, including and especially Mr Benjamin, and from thence the support of the *lurah* who is head of the four local villages including Bahowo. The fact that we could do nothing unless the village people were behind us was something that we were aware of even then, but only subsequently did we learn the full importance of this.

None of the people that we met on that or subsequent days

spoke any English, but the general atmosphere was friendly and positive, and through Mr A, who acted as interpreter if he was present at meetings, or by use of sign language (a skill at which we quickly had to become adept) we managed to make each other understood. We had reason to be optimistic regarding our obtaining the consent of the necessary parties. We checked into the nearest local hotel, and talked long into the night about the possibilities and pitfalls of that which we were about to attempt, none of the possibly negative aspects dampening our enthusiasm for our intended new life. It seems clear now, retrospectively, that in order to take on a challenge such as we were about to, it is essential to have that 'gut feeling' of knowing that this is what you want. This can become the only thing to sustain you through times of doubt and difficulty, which will (and did, for us) inevitably follow.

And of course there were and are two of us, and we had to be certain that we were both equally committed to the idea. Neither of us, we are now sure, would have seen the project through to its completion alone, and in fact in all probability could never have started it. We had been together long enough and so by now knew each other well enough to keep the faith in times of difficulty. If one of us was having a bad time, the other would be there to steer the ship, so to speak, and although we will not for the next few chapters talk much about 'us' again, it is true to say that in our experience and looking back from our now happy and contented situation, there are times when only deep love can keep you going.

In any case, to return to our story, we revisited the site the next day, partly to reconfirm our first impressions, and to see whether village discussions had resulted in any conclusion being reached, one way or the other. In the event, all of the village elders were in favour of our buying the land and building a tourist lodge, as it would, they said, raise the status of the village and provide employment for the villagers, both in the short term during the building work, and in the longer term, as of course we would need staff to run the place.

At the time we were aware of only one man who had reservations. He was called Marwin (later to be known by us as Marvelous Marwin). He lived in a bamboo house on the land and also had some banana trees planted thereupon, and we had to agree, before final consent would be given, to move his house to another location and compensate him for the loss of his bananas. This latter was a financial transaction, and the former would involve a number of village men picking up his house and re-locating it elsewhere in the village, which we of course agreed to, and it was in due course done.

Thus agreed, there was much smiling and shaking of hands; we had our agreement, and everything would follow from there. It is difficult for us now, given all that has occurred since that day, to really project ourselves back to our first feelings and impressions of our being about to buy land and eventually, we supposed, live in a foreign country, particularly one so foreign to us as Indonesia. Now it seems perfectly natural for us to be here, but then, in truth, we had not the least idea of what we were about to embark upon, other than that it was something extraordinary for both of us. Quite how extraordinary we did not find out until somewhat later. We were to re-enter the twilight zone many times in the next few months and years.

We subsequently learned that there was only one permanently dissenting voice in the village, who came out against our ideas, and that he was run out of the village. His house stays empty to this day.

5

The Building of Bahowo Lodge

Traditionally, ownership of all land in Sulawesi has been passed down through the generations. In the case of Bahowo village, it was Aris's grandfather who first settled in and staked his claim to the land, he who built the first house, and he who gave it its name. He then would have given areas of land to his children and any incomers to the village, who in turn would have passed this land on to their children, and so on. All of this was done before the land had any actual monetary value, its value being rather in its location within the settlement and access to local resources, and it was also done without the encumbrance or inconvenience of any official mapping or paperwork, the boundaries of the various plots of land being marked by trees, rocks and other natural markers, together with the general knowledge and acceptance of who owned what.

This would have to change once the 'Western people' moved in, since as foreigners we cannot own Indonesian land in our own right, but must do so via the legal entity of a foreign investment company, which we eventually set up in our joint names. To do this we would need a land certificate, which would bear the name of an Indonesian who would also have a small shareholding in the company. We will for now pass over the further complexities of all of this, but suffice to say that we first had to produce a land certificate in the name of Aris, which would allow our newly set up company to officially buy the land from him. This was duly done, the process taking several months and therefore in part running concurrently with the building of the lodge, and nothing more need be said of it save that it was just a part of the much larger and more complex process involving various government departments in Manado and Jakarta. Mr A undertook this work on our behalf, both of setting up the business, and becoming the 'name' on our land certificate. It was only later, once things had turned bad between us that this became significant, something that we will deal with later in our story.

In the meantime, we had to turn our minds to what we would build once the land was ours. One of the pieces that fell into place for us during this whole enterprise is that one of our oldest and dearest friends in England, a certain Mr Martin Evans, is an architect, and it was to him that we turned for advice. He and his wife Jill had been friends of ours since we had both bought our first flats in the same block during our years in Brighton, when Paula was studying at Sussex University. In the end, seeing that we had no idea how to proceed, he took on the whole project, and contrived eventually, after a few meetings at their then house in the New Forest, to design a beautiful lodge without ever having visited the location. Instead he relied upon sketches, photographs and any generally useful information that we could provide: 'The ocean is over there, the mountains are kind of in that direction, and there is a sort of sloping bit over here… oh, and try to avoid this coconut tree,' was the gist of it. In the event it was several years before he first came to visit us and see his design in its built and completed state, as he is rather reluctant to take long-haul flights, and we believe that he is generally pleased with the results.

So it was that in the following May of 2001 we returned to Sulawesi once more, armed with drawings and ready to begin the next phase of the process, which was to find somebody to build us a lodge. This potentially tricky process was in the event taken out of our hands, and so made easy for us. There is no equivalent to the Yellow Pages in Manado, and of course there was no internet service at the time, and indeed no concept of competitive tendering, so the villagers together with Mr A contrived to find our builder, who was duly summoned from Manado. In this way did 'Mr Yan' become our head builder. He took us to see a couple of houses that he had built, which looked okay, and to his credit he did try to tell us how much the contract was likely to cost, a figure that bore no resemblance to the amount we eventually paid him, but this appears to be true of building projects the world over.

The first thing you must do when building anything in this part of Indonesia is to organize and carry out the *pertama batu*, or 'first stone' ceremony. This involves the laying of the first foundation stone of a new building, during which the house is blessed, to ward off evil spirits. In order for this to be effective, we, as the owners, would need to be present during this ceremony, so the first foundation trench was laid, and the ceremony was carried out during the same visit, so that building work could commence before our return to England and carry on in our absence. The village priest was also present, and such other village elders who could attend. Each of us in turn laid a stone onto a mortar bed, whilst prayers and blessings were being said by the priest. Afterwards everybody had a nice cup of tea. Thus it was that we witnessed and were involved in the very first phase of construction of our lodge, a moment of great significance for us. If I may paraphrase the late Sir Winston Churchill (something that I am not generally given to doing), this was not the end, nor was it the beginning of the end, but it was, perhaps, the end of the beginning. Finally, our plans had begun to take on a third dimension.

Locally there is also the practice of pouring alcohol onto the topmost part of the building, once construction has reached this stage. Thus will the house be made a happy one, and those that dwell therein will have good fortune. You must also fly the Indonesian flag from the top of the building during construction, as this will mean that 'everything is all right'. We had a flag, so everything was all right.

During this visit we also had to set about the business of ordering the first building materials. All brick and concrete buildings in Sulawesi are built in essentially the same way: steel-reinforced concrete pillars support a concrete slab which forms the floor between the storeys (the decorative wooden ceilings are then suspended from the concrete floor above), and the gaps between the pillars are filled in with brick to form the walls, which are not, in fact, structural. Having been intimately involved in the construction of gardens during our former years, we were used to selecting from a variety of different brick types. In Indonesia, a brick is a brick, and the walls are always in any case rendered with sharp sand and cement. Since we are fairly certain that further details of the construction will not be of particular interest to the majority of people, we will pass over this aspect, and concentrate on the more human elements of the building work. Suffice to say that we took delivery of the first materials during this visit, and thereafter would send monthly payments to Mr A so that the building work and administration could and would continue after our return to England.

Mr Yan, it turned out, was a drunkard. He would get completely hammered each evening on local palm wine, and after sundown could be seen wandering around the building site in a drunken stupor, or collapsed in some alcohol-induced torpor amongst the brick rubble and building materials. In the morning he would emerge somehow for the day's work, during which he would smoke about five packs of the very Indonesian clove cigarettes, or *kretek*. To see him awake and without a cigarette in his mouth was a rare sight indeed. He was, for all that, a thoroughly decent man, had a voice like gravel, a ready smile and was, as it turned out, a very good builder, and for these reasons we grew to like him very much.

Incidentally, this may be as good a time as any to digress briefly and say something of the aforementioned palm wine, which we may meet again sometimes during this narrative. The basic model is known as Captikus, *Cap* meaning brand, and *tikus* meaning mouse or rat, so it is 'Mouse Brand'. It tastes okay, after a fashion, and better after a few glasses. It costs about 50 pence a bottle, which makes it affordable for and very popular amongst the village men. (The village women seldom drink alcohol.) The more refined version is known as 'Pinaraci', which is the same stuff only with some locally grown spices added, and as such is reckoned to have medicinal qualities. The *kretek* were invented and developed some one hundred years ago as a prevention against and cure for chest ailments (it's the cloves, you know). However, one only has to smoke one to realize that their curative qualities are perhaps overstated, since one feels as though one has sucked on an exhaust pipe. The village men smoke them all the time, for which they have my deepest respect.

It was our policy during the building work, and has remained so with subsequent construction projects, to employ Bahowo people wherever possible, only employing outside labour where a specialist skill was required. So that the reader may gain some impression of an Indonesian building site, the builders and labourers sleep on the job, and since there are no concrete mixers or other mechanical building aids, there tend to be a lot of them. We thus had a gang of builders and labourers on site six days and nights a week. On the seventh night, unless they were Bahowo people, they would depart for their various villages with their week's wages, on the other six they would curl up on cardboard sheets in whichever room they were building at the time. They work in T-shirts, shorts and flip-flops (or no shoes at all), protective clothing being something that happens on another planet. The whole affair is a complete mess of cement dust, cigarette smoke, heat, noise and general chaos, but it began to smell and seem like progress.

One or both of us would visit the site about every three or

four months, as time and money would allow, since we were still very much working in England as the building proceeded. During the early stages, when there was no shelter to be had, we would retire at night to the local hotel, and later, once rooms began to emerge from the chaos, we would camp out in the building site and cook our meals on a single-burner stove. We became experts at one-pan cooking, and during the months of primary construction, various members of our family and friends would visit with us for 'holidays'. That is, those relations and friends who did not object to spending their holidays sleeping in rooms without doors, or to showering or washing the dishes by means of a hosepipe.

We retain many lasting memories and impressions of our first visits to the lodge. We had and still have a very large mango tree in the garden, under which we would erect temporary wooden seats and sit for long, hot tropical evenings with the village people, smoking cigarettes and drinking coffee, laughing and getting to know each other. We were, after all, the first white people with whom they would have had contact, and they were keen to learn what manner of beings were about to come and live amongst them, what it is like where we come from, how cold it really gets, and so on. Perhaps we should emphasize how little the people of Bahowo and villages like it know of the outside world. They seldom travel far from their own villages and families; few have travelled to other parts of Indonesia, and never would they have been beyond its borders. So that you may gain some kind of impression of how these people look, they are for the most part much smaller and slighter of build than those of us of Caucasian extraction, with mid-brown to dark skin, dark brown eyes and normally straight, always jet-black hair. It is generally true that in certain parts of Indonesia such as Irian Jaya the people have much curlier hair, and thus it is hereabouts considered good to have straight hair. As one might expect, attempts are sometimes made, particularly by young people, to lighten their hair or change its colour in some way, always with aesthetically disastrous consequences. Conversely, many women from the west would pay good money to imitate the beautiful, shiny black hair which is standard issue here. All babies in the village are born with a full head of thick black hair and when the local people see pictures of newborn European babies they laugh hysterically at their baldness, once we have explained that the babies do not have any illness or deformity which has caused their unfortunate baldness – it is just they way they are.

Anyway, in this most informal of settings we began to learn their language, and they to learn ours. This learning process began in the most elementary ways, for example we would point at a tree and then we would speak the name in our respective languages. Verbs would be learned by imitating the action of the verb in question, for example eating, sleeping and so on. 'I' could be indicated by pointing at oneself, and 'we' by pointing at everybody. We were really back to the basics of language and communication, and it was enormous fun for all concerned. Indeed the most abiding memories of this period are of laughter – we never seemed to stop laughing at and with each other, and these were magical times.

Eventually, as the building work moved on and water pumps, electric lights and so on were installed and wired up, we had a generator on site for occasional electricity. The beast of a machine was extremely noisy and churned out diesel fumes approximately equivalent to a small power station, so we used it only when absolutely necessary. Nevertheless, these were good times, and to see our lodge being built around us was an experience never to be forgotten. We had also by this time forged strong relations with the village folk, who would often bring us plates of *pisang goreng* (fried bananas) and other delicious local dishes, such as *nasi goreng* (fried rice) and mie sup (noodle and vegetable soup), since they did not believe that the silly English couple could possibly look after themselves. Deep bonds of friendship were formed then, which have never been broken.

During subsequent visits, as the building process continued, we were wired into the mains electricity grid, the air-conditioning units were installed and things became very much more comfortable. We even by then had the luxury of some doors and windows.

One critical stage of building came when pouring the concrete for the first floor (which is also the ceiling for the ground floor). This involved laying a huge expanse of 150-mm-thick reinforced concrete, which must be laid in one go to avoid any weak joints in the construction. The work required some forty men, some mixing the concrete, others forming a human chain to pass the concrete up a ladder in buckets and across the working area, and still others collecting the empty buckets and throwing them back down to the mixers. At the end of the chain was one man with a length of wood, tamping and screeding the concrete into its final place. The work commenced before dawn, at about 4 a.m., and continued long into the morning, and once finished the day's wages were handed out, along with the requisite quantities of palm wine and *kretek*, and everybody took the rest of the day off. At dawn the next morning as we walked on the newly laid concrete floor and saw our views over the ocean for the first time, we began to think that perhaps this was a good thing that we were doing.

Scaffolding in this part of the world is constructed of bamboo that has been collected from the forest and tied together with hemp rope. On this scaffolding very thin boards are (sometimes) laid, and upon said boards all work is carried out on the upper storeys and roof. Despite the seemingly haphazard nature of this arrangement, as far as we are aware there were no accidents of note during construction, and we have, during this and subsequent building projects, gained great respect for Indonesian builders in general. They work hard, accurately and diligently, and their genius is in creating strong, beautiful buildings with hardly any equipment. They can make something from whatever is lying around, creating a screwdriver from a bent nail, or a broom from a piece of branch, and in this way, after some eighteen months, and a few more trips to Bahowo by one or both of us, we had the bones of a building.

There were, as one might expect, deviations from the original plans, and some things got lost somewhat in translation. Mr Yan had never worked from architectural plans before, and so misunderstandings were perhaps inevitable. Thus at certain stages we had doors where there should have been windows, and visa versa, and had to make adjustments in progress. Martin, our architect, had drawn one circular window at a certain focal point in the building, which in the end became a square window. We had designed some of the upper rooms with French windows, which were to have iron railings across the opening. Mr Yan clearly thought that doors that lead nowhere must be a mistake, and put windows in instead. And then in addition to this we had certain cultural differences to overcome; for example, it is considered very bad luck in Indonesia to have the front and back doors of a room directly facing each other, so some of the doors had to be moved around to allow for this. Probably the most lasting legacy of this cultural diversity, however, is in the height of our ceilings. Martin had designed the rooms to a height of 2.7 metres, quite acceptable in a Western house, where heat conservation is a major factor. In Indonesia, however, where heat dispersal is rather the order of the day, much higher and cooler ceilings are the norm, and so we have a room height of 3.3 metres with dropped ceilings. This is perfectly okay, although it has meant that consequently our staircases are rather steeper than one would normally expect, and our guests and visitors to the lodge sometimes comment upon this fact.

Mr A was at this time still generally around if we were not, but he had no experience of building work. We therefore had to deal directly with Mr Yan, who spoke not a word of English, and we at this stage still spoke very little useful Indonesian. We therefore became adept at putting our thoughts and feelings across to each other by means of scratching things on walls, sign language and whatever other means were at our disposal. If everybody was smiling at the end of a meeting, then it had been a good meeting, all was well and the building work could proceed.

There was some excitement, particularly amongst the village children, when the plumbing began to be installed. None of them had ever seen a tap before, and would often visit the building site, which was at this time still open house to the villagers, just for the experience of turning on the taps and watching the water come out.

Eventually by these various means we had a building, with which we were generally very pleased, and nothing, it seemed, could progress very much further until we were actually living in Indonesia. What we thus had to decide was when to do this, since, respectively, notice had to be handed in and business run down to a stop. The choices as it seemed to us at the time were to stay working in England for another year or so, thereby saving more capital for our venture, or to leave more or less immediately. Over a few glasses of wine one night (most of our decisions, you may have noticed, seem to be taken under the influence of alcohol, which is perhaps not an entirely good thing) we decided upon the latter. After all, as we convinced ourselves, there is probably never a point at which one decides that one has enough money, when there is always the possibility of accumulating more of it. Another aspect that influenced the timing of our departure was our Belgian Shepherd dog, Buru, (his full name was Samburu, named after a tribe and place in Africa where we had spent a wonderful holiday some years previously) who had been our faithful companion for some sixteen years. He was getting old, and we resolved not to go while he was still alive. I would take him to work each day in the Land Rover, and our daily walks were always a joy. The day he finally died was without doubt one of the saddest of our lives, and, aside from our families and friends, he was our last emotional tie, so to speak, with what had already begun to seem like our old life.

6

The Finding of Furniture

About two more trips were needed to buy and set up the making of furniture and fittings for the lodge, before it could be regarded as in any way habitable. Our carpenter at the time was based in Manado, although subsequently we have used village carpenters, Marvellous Marwin being amongst them. With each trip we would fill suitcases up to and above our weight allowance with bed linen, curtains, towels, napkin rings and many other items that could not be bought in Manado, and about one spare T-shirt each. Even knives and forks had to be imported in this way, as Manado people do not use knives, preferring to eat with fork and spoon; in any case, cutlery available at the time in Manado was of poor quality and tended to bend if used with too much gusto.

Traditionally, Indonesians have used wood, bamboo and rattan to furnish their homes; however, this has been increasingly replaced by plastic, in all forms and colours. Thus it was that our first furniture at the lodge was plastic, which we quickly purchased as we needed somewhere to sit other than upon the floor, pending the arrival of more robust and aesthetically pleasing wooden pieces. The plastic was of poor quality, and if one sat down too heavily upon the chairs, the legs would tend to give way and one would oft times end up on the floor anyway, by rather undignified means. Even if one managed to sit without incident, the addition of further weight such as a cup of tea would tend to tip the balance in favour of gravity, and sudden movements were at all times to be avoided. Such chairs were doubtless manufactured for use by Indonesian people, who are, almost without exception, smaller and lighter than those of us of European extraction, and tend to be more delicate in their movements. Incidentally we also, apparently, slam doors, which was something we learned when doors had begun to appear about the lodge. We would move from room to room closing doors in what we thought was a perfectly natural manner, and our Indonesian friends and staff would assume that we must be in bad temper, when in fact we were of a perfectly contented frame of mind.

In any case, the plastic had to go, and so whilst the orders for timber furniture were being fulfilled, we set about the task of finding alternatives. This usually happened more by luck than judgment, as was the case when one day we were driving along a most unprepossessing road in a very rural location, and we happened upon a workshop within which worked an old man who specialized in making beautiful furniture from Chinese bamboo. We bought all that he had on the spot, and ordered more. He worked alone, however, and all subsequent furniture, whilst beautifully crafted by his skilled hands, took a long time to come. He eventually died, and we have since failed to find a craftsman of his calibre.

We also, at around the same time, found a small shop in the backstreets of downtown Manado that sold rattan chairs and tables. Only a few were on display, hanging rather precariously from the rafters by string, but further enquiry revealed that there was a workshop elsewhere where the furniture was made, and so it was that we found our source of fine rattan furniture, and have become devoted if infrequent customers ever since. In the same way, in more recent times, we have found a stained-glass work-shop, from where we have commissioned some work (of a nonreligious nature, by the way), and a shop specializing in picture framing and atrocious aluminium shelving that also, as we found out quite by chance, keeps a few original oil paintings rolled up in the dark recesses of the establishment. We have since bought and framed several of these paintings, and they now adorn the walls of Bahowo Lodge. Manado and Sulawesi in general give up their treasures only reluctantly.

Also on display on the walls of the lodge are beautiful ceramic dolphins, seahorses and lizards. We have some English friends who work in ceramics, and during the early days of the lodge, pre- and post-construction, they would sometimes visit us. On one such occasion they came with ceramic pieces, which they had designed and made for us, and set them on our walls. All of the pieces were designed, formed, cut into smaller parts, glazed and fired before being brought over in suitcases and reassembled on site, the dolphins being more than a metre long and the lizards and seahorses only somewhat less. We made a copy of the dolphin design, and now there are two of them, cut from black and white ceramic tiles, at the bottom of our swimming pool.

The best furniture hereabouts is to be found in Gorontalo. Gorontalo is a town mid-way along the peninsula that forms North Sulawesi, too far, given the condition of the roads and general difficulties of transporting goods, to be of any practical use for those such as ourselves living in the Manado area. But that is where they make the best furniture, and, apparently, the best of everything else. It became a cliché that if something was not available in Manado, it could always be found in Gorontalo. Musical instruments are apparently no exception, and when I decided one day that I would like to obtain and learn to play a banjo (having already learned to play the guitar passably well), we were instantly directed to Gorontalo; apparently the Muslims there play them. To this day we cannot help imagining Muslims walking the streets of Gorontalo playing the banjo, and Gorontalo has taken on a mythical status in our minds.

It should be said that this was borne more out of a desire not to disappoint than a wish to deceive, since Indonesians hate to fall short of supplying what is required or wished for. To say that whatever item was in question was available, but not here, was thus a neat sidestep.

We have still never been to Gorontalo (nor, incidentally, have I ever bought a banjo) and neither have most people from Manado, but those who have say that it is but an average town with nothing much to recommend it. Certainly the furniture is nothing out of the ordinary, and nobody has come back reporting a superfluity or large array of stringed instruments. We will probably never go; imagine finding the lost city of Atlantis, only to discover that it looks like Croydon.

7

A New Life Begins

At the English end, our furniture and other worldly goods were distributed amongst our families and friends, as we had decided to let our cottage as an unfurnished accommodation. The irony of this was that during previous trips to other parts of Indonesia we had shipped back some stunning pieces of Indonesian furniture and ceramic work, and despite our best efforts, we were unable to find a way of getting these back to our part of Sulawesi. We could ship a container as far as Singapore, but thereafter things became complicated, and we could find no way to transport anything large as far as Manado. So they would have to stay in England, and we have thus far been unable to find anything like them locally. Our cottage, once empty, was duly cleaned and handed over to the letting agent, our financial affairs were put in some kind of order and, on 13th August 2003 we said goodbye, without much ceremony, to our old life, since at the other end of a couple of flights lay our new one.

The process thus far had been observed with a kind of resigned stoicism by our respective families. We are both the youngest siblings, and had always been the 'wild children', with a reputation for somewhat, shall we say, unconventional behaviour, and once we had set our minds on an idea we would tend to carry it through regardless of any advice to the contrary. This had led us into troubled waters at certain stages of our lives, but we are nothing if not survivors, and had always so far come up at least dusted off and scrubbed up if not perhaps the wiser for the experience, and ready to face the world anew. One is put in mind of the saying that fools rush in where angels fear to tread, but since one of us is an angel (Paula) and the other is a fool (that would be me), we always seem to have all the bases covered.

The fact that we had kept our house in England was something that was to help us sleep nights during times of doubt and tribulation. This is not a story of sell everything, use the life savings and re-mortgage the cat. Thus as we forged headlong into our new venture, without much idea or thought as to where it would eventually take us, and although everybody close to us probably expected that it would end in disaster, it would at least only be an Indonesian disaster. Any English disasters that we may have subsequently embarked upon would be another matter altogether, and could be considered in their own right. We, on the other hand, being, as we are, albeit in our very different ways, eternal optimists, knew that everything would work out okay in the end. This is, of course, no guarantee that it will.

The first question that we had to address upon our arrival in Bahowo was how to run a tourist lodge. In an ideal world we would have had a month or so to collect our thoughts and settle in before taking on this challenge. It is not, however, an ideal world and, as fate would have it, our local dive centre needed somewhere to put some guests. We therefore arrived to a houseful of them, thus launching our new careers as host and hostess in a jet-lagged, tired and rather confused and less than well-prepared condition.

We were, at least, spared the inconvenience of having to hire staff, as this had been taken care of by the village, and we were to have no choice in the matter. Nyoman was to be our housekeeper, Aris our driver and Sultje our cook and clothes-washer. Raymon, Nyoman's brother, was shortly to join us as second driver and gardener. From day one these people became enmeshed into our everyday existence, and with the exception of Aris (who left some five years later to be replaced by Tom, another brother of Nyoman and Raymon) and Feni, who joined the team and subsequently became our clothes-washer, still form the backbone of our working lives. Melda, Nyoman's wife, also helps out with the housekeeping and cooking when we are busy with a lodge full of guests.

This, as we would find out, was to be the way of things between us and the people of Bahowo. If the silly English didn't know where to buy, hire or borrow some vital component for running the lodge, then the village would step in and sort it out. If we needed additional help with a certain task or undertaking, then the requisite number of people would be appointed and would duly turn up to see to it that things got done, with no fuss or discussion. We had been adopted, our only job being to pay for the goods or services rendered, and this is as true today as it ever was.

We did experience some further language difficulties, since in the beginning none of our dear staff spoke any English, and our Indonesian vocabulary was approximately limited to 'today it is hot' (you were fairly safe with that one since every day it was hot), 'My name is Phil/Paula' and 'fried bananas'. It was time to improve our Indonesian, and in the meantime brush up on our sign language.

In any event, our first guests left without incident. We had proved to ourselves that we were able to play host and hostess without undue strain despite the 'newness' of the whole business, and we were able to spend the next few weeks and months gradually becoming better accustomed to our new roles, putting in place final refinements to the lodge, and generally trying to ensure the smooth running of our new establishment. This process is of course ongoing, and the business of improvement and the addition of new facilities, outbuildings and so on continues, but we did, at least, have somewhere from whence to start. We even dared to think that perhaps everything was going to be okay after all; however, as is the case with life in general, but perhaps especially in Indonesia, one should never assume anything.

8

A Difficult Beginning

A part of the process that we were required to undergo before becoming 'legal' in Indonesia was gaining the final stamp of approval from a certain minister, which would allow our newly set up company to do business here. We had paid our way through the various offices, from the *lurah*, or head of the four villages, to the *camat*, who is the district head of Bunaken, within which lies the village of Bahowo, to the mayor of Manado, to the governor's office, and so finally we arrived at the desk of 'Mr B', who shall be the only other person to otherwise remain nameless for purposes of this story.

We cannot emphasize too strongly the importance of signed, rubber-stamped letters and documents in Indonesia. It is something of a national obsession. With them, anything within reason is possible; without them, you sink without trace. That said, nothing is irreplaceable, and gaining said documents retrospectively is nearly always possible, it just becomes more expensive. So it is that having obtained our letter of approval from Mr B, it now remains safely under lock and key, only to be produced *in extremis*.

We have been and will continue to be careful during this tale to avoid the 'c' word when writing of government officials and others, but one thing of note occurred during our interview with

Mr B, which perhaps throws light on how Indonesians perceive their own system of government. For after the formalities were over, his staff had left the office and we were alone with Mr B, and whilst the requisite amount of cash was being passed across the table, he said, without hint of irony: 'There is no corruption here.' Having successfully overcome our strong desire to laugh, we were left to ponder these words, and have done so oft times since.

Thereafter our morning with Mr B passed off pleasantly enough; he offered to drive us to see his house, which is made entirely of coconut wood, and then suggested that we might go for lunch. The fact that he was driving himself caused his staff a good deal of consternation, since apparently this rarely if ever happens, and they followed in another car at a close distance.

We arrived nonetheless without incident at a fish restaurant in Manado, and so, in the end, did some twenty of his staff. A fine time was had by all, and at the end the unpaid bill was quietly slipped to our driver, for our attention, of course. There may be no corruption here, but there may be such a thing as a free lunch, after all.

Another of the early events to mark our first weeks in Bahowo was our parting company with Mr A. We had had a series of disagreements and misunderstandings, before and after our eventual arrival here, and in the end the situation became untenable. There is no need to recount specific instances here that caused our falling out, as these have no particular relevance to our story, but in large part it was caused by the general lack of accountability for the cash that we had been sending over from England before our arrival, and Mr A's perception of his role in the company. Things became very unpleasant between us, and were finally brought to a head one day when we went to collect some company documents from his house. He threatened Paula with violence, and then proceeded to pour petrol over our jeep and would probably have set fire to it had his wife not intervened. She then pointed out in no uncertain terms that, since the vehicle was parked only a metre or so away from their rather small but nevertheless new house, if the jeep exploded then it would probably reduce their home to a pile of rubble.

We left without further incident, with ourselves and our vehicle intact, but also without our documents.

So it was time for us to remove Mr A from our affairs. The problem for us was that once an Indonesian becomes integral to a business run by foreigners, it can be extremely difficult to remove them, certainly by the normal, legal channels. We did attempt this method, and visited the lawyer in Manado who had originally set up our company. In his offices we spent a morning going over the same ground in the time-honoured circular fashion, and he displayed the normal obsession with photocopies of documents, which bore no apparent relevance to the subject under discussion. We were back in the twilight zone, and eventually we could take no more and left, being none the wiser for the experience except in so much as it had become clear to us that we would need to find other means of severing our ties with Mr A.

We decided, therefore, that our best course of action would be to take advantage of the fact that Mr A had threatened us, and particularly Paula, with violence, and to report the incident to the police since, as we will discuss in a later chapter, in Indonesia violence against women is considered to be one of the worst of crimes.

And so it was that the next day we went to the police headquarters in Manado. Here we were introduced to Amelia, a high ranking official who has the ear of the police commissioner, who was to act as our interpreter and who has since become a genuine friend. We had, of course, to produce various and numerous documents before anything could be done, which required my returning to Bahowo whilst Paula gave statements and so on. As luck would have it our jeep broke down on the way, and I was forced to continue the journey by motorbike, but eventually all the required papers were assembled and the process could continue. In the end we were to spend some seven hours in the police headquarters, Mr A was summoned, and we had a long and protracted meeting with all present wherein it was decided that Mr A would not be allowed to see or make contact with us thereafter. A police 'minder' was allocated to us in case of further trouble, and this turned out to be Tom, who now works for us. In any case we had achieved our first intent, which was to begin the severance of ties with Mr A.

This was by no means to prove the end of our problems; in the first place, he still had certain documents of ours, which we would need to continue with the business, and for this we once again turned to Amelia.

In a later chapter we will make further reference to the role of the police in Sulawesi. They are a powerful institution, second only, for foreign people such as ourselves, to the Immigration Office (who are all-powerful), but for now suffice to say that it was to a certain branch of this fine institution that we turned for help, a somewhat covert branch of the police force called 'The Enforcers', which Amelia had told us of. (There must be a TV series in there somewhere.) Their job is to take care of business when all other avenues have been exhausted, and generally deal with the messy side of things. Probably the flying squad would be our English equivalent. Retrieving documents is apparently part of their job description, and their methods in such situations as ours are to visit the offending person three times. The first time they ask politely, the second time they ask with menaces, and the third time (if there is a third time) they do whatever needs to be done to see the job through. In this way they apparently have a fairly high success rate, and in any event we got most of our documents back. We paid handsomely for this service, since the police here will not act unless paid to do so, but we considered it money well spent. The enforcers had, after all, enforced.

One further event relating to this is worth recounting, which is that Amelia asked us if she and 'The Enforcers' could subsequently visit us at Bahowo Lodge for a kind of tea party to celebrate the retrieval of our documents. Of course we agreed (well you would, wouldn't you?) and we have an abiding image of several very large and menacing looking policemen sitting by our swimming pool drinking soft drinks and eating fairy cakes ('This is very nice fairy cake, thank you'). This, we feel, could only happen in Indonesia. After their departure, we had a phone call from Amelia to say that the policemen were disappointed that we had not offered them further remuneration for their trouble. We had paid officially, of course, but not unofficially, so a driver was dispatched with an envelope containing the requisite amount of rupiah, to put matters to rights.

We did see Mr A one more time, when he visited the Lodge with two 'lawyers', the intention of the visit presumably being to intimidate us. It soon became clear that they were not in fact lawyers, as when asked for a business card or office address they couldn't come up with anything, which rather stole their thunder and they left without further incident. They had not been gone two minutes when three large, white birds flew into the front wall of the lodge and died instantly. Nyoman and Raymon collected the dead birds and gave them to us, saying that these were our three enemies, that the problem was over and that we would never see them again. Spooky, you might say. This has turned out to be true, and we have since learned a great deal more about the symbolism and beliefs of Sulawesi people, which we will deal with in more detail in a later chapter.

This left us with one major, residual issue, which was that Mr A's name was still on our land certificate, a copy of which he had managed to retain despite the attentions of the enforcers. This gave him power that he could still use against us from a distance, and we needed to take action to counter this threat. The village once again stepped in on our behalf, and Mr Aris, Mr Benjamin, the village head, and Mr Karel, the then head of the four villages, duly went to the land registry office in Manado to remove Mr A's name from the land documents, and obtain a new certificate. Faxes were exchanged with Jakarta, where all

45

land records are ultimately kept, and within a few days we had a new 'name' on our land registration: that of Mr Aris. The small irony here, of course, is that it was from him that we bought the land in the first place, and he now, at least officially, owned the land once more, but in this way we made our position secure. It is perhaps worth noting that what we had done was effectively to circumvent any rightful, legal claim that Mr A had to the land, something that could never have happened, of course, under British law, but the system is rather more feudal and flexible in Indonesia, provided that the money is there to provide the flexibility.

While this process was underway, Mr A was attempting to secure a personal loan of an unspecified amount, and one would imagine at a very high rate of interest, using our land certificate as surety. This was without our knowledge or consent, and we discovered this fact only when the proposed lenders visited Bahowo to check on the authenticity of the certificate, and the existence of the lodge, which would have given it its value. The village elders were quick to come to our defence once more and explain the situation to the lenders, and thus was the transaction halted. Had it not been so, we would have lost our certificate to the loan 'company', which would have placed us in a highly vulnerable position, with at least a large loan to pay off before we could retrieve our certificate, and probably with unforeseeable consequences well beyond this.

It later transpired that Mr A was apparently also attempting to sell the land certificate to the Chinese, who constitute a small but powerful minority in Manado, and own most of the business there. Vehicles with darkened windows would pull up outside the lodge from time to time, stay a few minutes and drive away, and it all became rather like a bad movie. Whilst Mr A had no power, or more importantly, money, to come against us himself, had he been successful in selling the land certificate and we had come up against Chinese ownership of our land, things would have worked out very differently for us, and probably our venture would have been over before it had begun. In the event we beat him to the land registry office by some two days, and our new certificate was issued before the Chinese could take control.

Aris duly signed a document disclaiming any rights to the land that bore his name; we had thereby made our position as secure as it was possible to make it, and we had become wiser to the ways of our adopted country. We had learned, for instance, that whilst there is a deal of fuss made over documents, what is more important in the end is who is fighting your corner.

9

A Boundary Dispute

Whilst we are on the subject of land, we would like to convey the tale of how we have come to own, through the name of Nyoman our housekeeper, about a hectare of land in the centre of Bahowo village that we didn't at the time really want. This land is bordered on two sides by the back gardens of the village houses, on one side by jungle leading down to the sea, and on the fourth side by the gardens of Bahowo Lodge. It was this border that came to be in dispute. The land was empty aside from a few trees, mainly old coconut trees of perhaps a hundred years or so in age, which have since been cut down to make furniture for the lodge and build a house for Raymon. The word 'empty', it should be said, is used advisedly when describing land here, since in this lush, tropical environment the jungle quickly takes over.

The story begins at a time before we were living in Bahowo, but after completion of the main construction work to the lodge. At this time we were still only visiting every three months or so, and were concerning ourselves with the aforementioned matters of the making of furniture, final 'making good' of the building, swimming pool construction and beginning to clear and re-plant areas of the garden.

On one such visit, in May 2002, I happened to come alone, and was greeted at the lodge by five rather aggressive looking men with machetes, who said that we had our boundary markers in the wrong place, that they were all brothers, and by virtue of the fact that they owned the adjacent land, they in fact owned about a three-metre wide stretch of our garden. This would not have been a matter of great concern, since our gardens are quite large, but their taking the disputed land would effectively cut off our vehicular access to the lodge, something that, of course, they knew very well. It would also have cut off the pedestrian route to the village graveyard, which lies adjacent to what was still at the time their land, so the village people would have had no legal access thereto.

Having arrived in the usual jet-lagged and tired state, I was in no mood for an argument. In any case I was alone, there were five of them; they had machetes, I had a suitcase full of towels and bed linen. Hardly a fair fight then, had it come down to it, so I said that I would deal with the matter the next day. The fact that they had foreknowledge of my arrival was significant, since nobody apart from Mr A knew that I was coming on that day, and so it seems clear that he was somehow in league with the family, and stood to gain some financial benefit from this.

That evening I had discussions with the village elders, who once again found us a solution. We were to buy another much smaller adjacent plot of land that would give us an alternative route of access from the village road, and move our driveway accordingly. This is what we duly did, having first tested the water with the brothers to see if they would sell us back the disputed strip of land. Of course they would not, they would only sell us the whole plot at well above 'market prices', and so we left the matter there, eventually moved our driveway through the labours of the good men of Bahowo, and thought nothing more of it. We made it clear to the brothers that we were not interested in doing business with them, and never, in fact, contested their claim to the disputed land, since this would have been a long and protracted process. In any case our buying the additional smaller plot had other advantages for us, as we will see in a later chapter.

It was not until some three years later that we had a visitation from a small, wizened old lady, who announced herself as the mother of the brothers. It transpired that only three of them were her children, she also had two daughters, and that the family would like to sell us the once disputed plot of land, as her husband was very sick and the family needed cash to pay hospital bills. Our staff reminded her of the events that occurred the last time we had encountered her family (Indonesians have very long memories), for which she apologized and said that they were much nicer people these days. (I daresay the machetes were rusting in the cupboard by now, swords into ploughshares and all that.)

As we mentioned earlier, we were not particularly interested at that time in buying more land, so we asked her the price, which was somewhat reduced from the original figure, and said thank you but given prior events we were not interested in doing business with her. We gave her a cup of tea, however, as she was very old and it was brave of her to come unprotected and alone into the lion's den, so to speak. She came back a month or so later, to see if we had changed our minds, and it was on her third such visit that we agreed to go ahead with the purchase. By this time we could more or less name our price, and after all, land is land, and our buying it would forever protect our boundary. The other factor in our favour was that our positions had somewhat been reversed, since there was now no access onto her land except through our garden, or one of the village gardens, rendering it virtually useless to anybody else but ourselves.

In the event her husband died before the deal could go through, and it was then that things began to get strange. We had agreed a date and time to meet at the local *camat's* office to do the transaction, for it is the *camat*, or district head, who deals with land sales, being the equivalent to and having the power of a solicitor in such transactions. It was, as in most cases here, to be a cash transaction, so we arrived with a briefcase full of rupiah.

The *camat* had drawn up the documents for the family to sign, and the deal was due to proceed. This was, by the way, our second encounter with the machete-wielding sons, all of whom would have to sign the documents. This is very important, since unless all sons and daughters sign off on a land deal, any one of them who does not sign can at any time in the future lay claim to the land in question. We have known cases locally where people have bought land in good faith, built property or a resort on the land, only to lose ownership and therefore everything when a thereto unknown family member has made a claim against them. In a court of law, an Indonesian will always win against a foreigner, almost regardless of the circumstances.

In any case, returning to our meeting, it was at this point that the dear lady raised the price of the land, we said that we would not pay more than we had agreed, and after about an hour or so of circular Indonesian-style discussion we removed ourselves and our money from the negotiating table. The next day her eldest son dropped dead from no apparent causes, and word began to get about that we had put a curse on the family.

She came back to the lodge a couple of weeks later, assuring us that if we were still willing to buy the land there would, this time, be no last-minute price increases, and in fact we said that we would pay less this time around as she had caused us considerable inconvenience the last time. This agreed, we duly met again at the *camat's* office, and she tried to raise the price again. Negotiations broke down immediately, we left the office once more, and her second eldest son, apparently in a state of perfect health, passed away the next day. Our magic was clearly very strong, and could not be countered, and so shortly thereafter, on the third attempt, the sale went through without further hitch or hindrance, and we had become the proud owners of a bit more of Indonesia. We feel, in fact, that the last surviving son would probably have given us the land for free had we asked for it, but we paid nonetheless, and have seen none of the remaining family since. Just to complete the story, we subsequently bought another much smaller piece of land which runs from the village road to the new land, to give us vehicular access thereto. This land had a house upon it belonging to a certain Mr Judas (quite how he came by this unfortunate name is unclear, and he is also known locally as 'Mr Problem for Jesus'), which had to be moved to a new location. We had visualized the dismantling and reassembling of the building, which was built in the traditional way with wood and bamboo, but in fact, as we now know, the house was supported by struts beneath and was manually lifted by several village men in its intact state and placed elsewhere in the village as seemed desirable. A more literal meaning perhaps to the term 'moving house'.

In any event the new land has subsequently in fact proved very useful, and we have built houses for Raymon and Tom upon it. We have also sold off a section to an English friend, who is at the time of writing in the process of building a beautiful Minahasa-style house, with a view to eventually spending at least part of her time in Bahowo. To bring matters up to date, we have also recently planted about 600 mahogany, chempaka, cinnamon and other trees on the land, so it will, we hope, in years to come become a cool, shady forest.

So what we learned from this episode is that land is land, magic is magic, and there is to this day a three-metre dog-leg in our garden wall to testify to the above events.

And so, dear reader, we come to the conclusion of the first part of our book, which has seen us arrive and become established as citizens of Bahowo village. Throughout the events recounted in the first chapters, we were at the same time learning how to run a tourist lodge, and to respond to the needs and wishes of our guests. We will recount tales of this in a later chapter.

All of the above events, of course, occurred in the context of our having moved to a place where much of the time we had little or no idea what was going on, who we should and should not trust, what were the rules of engagement, or how best to proceed, and we are forever indebted to those people who helped us through our early months in Indonesia. For these had been strange times, and we felt as though we had been on a kind of emotional roller coaster, where despair would be replaced by joy or frustration by relief in the course of a single day. We know of the adage 'What doesn't kill you will make you stronger', and if this is true then, since we are still very much alive, we came out of our 'baptism by fire' the stronger and wiser for having been through it.

In the course of the next few chapters you will meet us again from time to time in various contexts, and we will return to our own story later on. Before we do so, however, we would like to devote some time to introducing you to and imparting some tales of the people of Bahowo, and describing our impressions of some elements of the lives of the people amongst whom we have come to live.

10

Meet the Staff

It would perhaps be disingenuous of us not to devote a few pages of our narrative to our staff, so if you will allow us, we will begin this next part of our book by briefly introducing them.

As we have mentioned previously, our staff were allocated to us by the village people of Bahowo, before we arrived to have any say in the matter. This was entirely appropriate, since, despite Paula's vast and wide experience in the area of human resources and staff selection, we would have had not the least idea how to go about selecting from those villagers willing to work for us (which was most of them), since the normal process of interviews and so on was not open to us in view of the language difficulties. It is incidentally also a peculiarity of the Indonesian employment system that we, as foreigners, cannot hire or dismiss staff directly. This must be done by an Indonesian. In any event, aside from having the basic skills of driving and so on, nobody in the village had previously had any direct contact with tourists or 'Western people' in general, and certainly, like us, had no experience of working in the tourist industry. We would all be starting from scratch.

Of our original staff all but one person, Aris, who left to return to his traditional trade as a fisherman, have remained with us since starting work at the Bahowo Lodge. We remain on good terms with Aris, and his wife, Sultje, has been our cook since day one, providing delicious Indonesian fare for us and our guests. Indeed since she has worked for us, and cooked many thousands of individual meals, it is true to say that we have never had a single complaint. From time to time, when guests of Bahowo Lodge meet those from other resorts on the dive boats, said other guests will come for their evening meal at the lodge, and will thereafter often return to eat with us, sometimes every night of their holiday. In her own quiet and modest way she has, one might say, built up an international reputation for her Indonesian, and specifically Sangihe, cuisine. As a rule she cooks alone, although if the number of guests in residence gets too great, as is frequently the case, then she will call in additional help from the village women.

We have always had an 'open kitchen' policy at the lodge, and our guests will often spend time with Sultje in the early evenings, picking up advice on particular recipes, or just watching her perform her magic. In my opinion, eating her *dabu-dabu* (chilli sauce), or her *sos-kacang* (sweet peanut sauce) are other-worldly experiences in their own right. We have several labour-saving devices in the lodge kitchen, which variously chop, grind, mix or otherwise alter the state of foodstuffs. Sultje rarely if ever uses them, preferring the traditional methods. For example, she has a large *lisum*, or hollowed-out grinding stone, in which she mixes and grinds the ingredients for her *dabu-dabu*, using a heavy stick about a metre long. She prefers to spend time chopping vegetables and so on into the perfect size or shape for the dish she is cooking, rather than use a food processor. Mostly she now uses our conventional cooker, but oft times, especially when cooking saté, she will cook the meat or vegetables outside, over a fire of coconut shells, which gives the food its distinctive flavour. All in all she is a gem, and aside from her occasional brushes with our guests in the kitchen, she prefers to remain quietly in the background, and watches proceedings at the lodge from a distance.

The other three of our permanent staff are all brothers, of the Bangsuil family. Nyoman, our housekeeper, was the first to be introduced to us. We had in fact met him previously, as he was one of the labourers working on the construction of the lodge, but at that time neither we nor he had any idea that he would become so integral to our future. He had previously worked mainly in construction, but had for two years been a professional boxer, and perhaps in contradiction to this is the most skilled of the brothers at healing, massage and traditional medicine. In the course of the various building projects that we have undertaken since we have lived here, which generally happen when we have no guests in residence, he has become a competent builder in his own right, and we nowadays at such times hand him a drawing or give instructions, and leave him to coordinate materials and any additional labour that we may need to employ from the village. He also acts as coordinator and contract manager for our occasional village projects, about which we write later, and for the various tradesmen who help us to maintain the lodge. He is also the link between us and our sponsored schoolchildren (more on this later as well), and he generally keeps a watch in the village as to which families may need our help.

His main role, however, as regards the daily running of the lodge, is as our housekeeper and keeper of the keys, and in this latter role he is also in charge of internal security. He and his wife, Melda, are very diligent with money, and largely due to this fact they have built themselves a very nice brick house in the village. Indeed, visitors to Bahowo will often ask Nyoman what line of work has allowed him to build such a house, to which he always and simply replies 'cleaning service'. This typifies his rather dry humour, and he is by nature a solid, hard-working, totally reliable individual, of quite serious disposition.

Raymon is the older brother of Nyoman, and he joined the team shortly after the lodge had opened. Ostensibly and origin-ally he was our gardener, and in this capacity he has over the years created for us beautiful tropical gardens. In his horticultural capacity he has also been responsible for planting and managing our newly created 'forest', and has the general role of groundkeeper and outside maintenance man, including taking care of the swimming pool.

He also holds a driving licence, and originally performed the role of second driver alongside his gardening duties. Since the departure of Aris, however, he has become our main driver and tour guide, and takes our guests on weekly tours to Minahasa, Tangkoko Forest, Manado, and so on. He looks after the maintenance of our vehicles, and is also responsible for our monthly administration, guest registration, staff social security payments etc. and is generally our main man in town. He is also our 'airport man' and has spent many hours of his working life waiting at Manado airport for our newly arrived guests. Another of his no less important jobs is to see us and our friends and guests safely home after our nights spent in the restaurants and nightclubs of Manado, be this late at night or, as is more often the case, in the small hours of the morning.

He is the most artistic and aesthetically creative of our staff, as befits his role as our gardener. He has the temperament to match, and when on form has, shall we say, a well-developed sense of humour. He tends to have more 'interface' with our guests, particularly in his capacity as tour guide, and his outgoing personality is well suited to this part of his work. He also has a big house, by village standards, which is situated in a beautiful location on our 'new land'.

Quite recently Tom, the youngest of the Bangsuil brothers, has joined the team, and has fit comfortably into the role of our second driver and tour guide, sometimes night security man (although the need for any form of security here is questionable) and in general he is the 'link man' between internal and external matters. He is also excellent with our guests and guest relations in general, and so has quickly become an invaluable and integral part of the lodge. He is also, incidentally, an excellent chess player, and he and I have some titanic battles over the chessboard when time allows.

Via Nyoman and now Tom, we offer a massage service at Bahowo Lodge. In the first instance we had to introduce Nyoman to the concept of giving massage for pleasure and relaxation, as opposed to healing. The first time that one of our guests asked for a massage, he first wanted to know where the problem lay. Since, as we told him, there was no problem, there seemed to him no point in doing the massage, so we told him to start at one end and work up to the other, and if he came upon a problem then he could heal it. This he understood, and has since become adept at finding problems, many of them 'old' problems, that our guests did not necessarily even know they had. We have since built him a traditional, purpose-made massage room in the garden, and he regularly gives massages to our guests, who speak very highly of his skills. Paula is a regular visitor; I have only been 'done' once by Nyoman, which remains my one and only experience of massage. I found the whole business so relaxing that I was asleep within minutes and missed the rest of the process, but I awoke feeling much the better for it. He is from time to time called upon to undertake curative massage as well. In particular our guests will sometimes develop minor lower-back problems from carrying scuba tanks whilst diving, and owing to his ability to discover and take care of 'old' or longer term problems, many of our guests have left Bahowo Lodge with fewer problems than when they arrived.

Melda, Nyoman's wife, provides invaluable assistance during busy times as a second housekeeper and cook, particularly when we have to prepare twenty breakfasts by 7.30, as is sometimes the case when our guests are numerous and diving early. Feni, her mother, is our clothes-washer.

To work in the tourist industry requires an extraordinary commitment over and above that required for 'normal' work, and when we have guests in residence our staff work seven days a week, and must be on call from early morning and often until late into the evening. All of them, in their own way, have proved themselves to be totally devoted and dedicated to Bahowo Lodge, and without this devotion and dedication it would be quite impossible for us to provide service to our guests. Aside from matters of work, they have all become close personal friends, and we are intimately involved with them and their families.

11

Culture and Culture Shocks

Bahowo, as we have mentioned before, was originally founded as a fishing community in 1953, and fishing is still the main occupation for many of the families. Most families also have an area of land on the borders of the village, put over to coconut, banana or clove plantations, and there are local communal areas of rice paddies. The main vegetable- and rice-growing areas of the region are, however, in the highlands, the lowland and coastal agriculture being mainly subsistence farming, with some goods being sold weekly at the markets in Manado. In the season, spices such as cloves and nutmeg are laid out to dry on rice sacks by the side of the roads, this being the hottest place available. The almost incredible value of these spices to the Dutch traders in former times may be no more, but the methods of production remain unchanged.

The coconuts are harvested twice a year, and processed into 'copra' by twice smoking the flesh of the coconut, before it is sold on for processing and eventually for the cosmetics and other industries. Nowadays, some of the young men work on the construction sites in Manado, which is a rapidly growing and developing city. For the girls, there are now career opportunities in commerce and banking, but since for village families the costs of sending their children on to further education are completely prohibitive, these opportunities have not hitherto reached the villages. There are two exceptions to this general rule in Bahowo, since we have been able, with the aid of donations from our guests, to put Ingrid and Trefina, two of our village girls, through university courses in Manado. They are the first girls from the village ever to do so, and Ingrid is now a teacher in the Bahowo primary school, while Trefina works in a bank. More will be written about our 'social projects' in a later chapter.

Some houses in the village are of brick construction, but the majority of them are still made from timber and bamboo, materials that can be obtained from the forest. Traditionally the roofs are made from palm leaves, although more commonly nowadays they are of the ubiquitous corrugated tin. Each house has one reception room or lounge with one or two small bedrooms, the kitchen always being out the back, usually outdoors with a covered tin or palm roof. There are often no internal doors, sometimes no doors at all and no glass as a rule, thus avoiding the 'greenhouse effect' and aiding ventilation. Often the only electrical appliance in a house will be a single light bulb, although some houses now have televisions (but no refrigerators or other white goods). Only a few houses have electric meters, from which several other houses in the locale run cables, and the houses, with a very few exceptions, do not have toilets. The villagers will often take 'showers' two or three times a day, which are of the traditional *mandi*, or bucket and scoop, variety, there being no running water in the village houses (the only source of water being stand pipes along the village road). Prior to the advent of the stand pipes which were installed in 2005, the washing of clothes had always been done in the local stream. The women (for it is almost invariably the women who wash their family's clothes) will often wash the clothes that they are wearing at the same time, whilst still wearing them, often disappearing under a layer of soap bubbles. Yet another example of Indonesian pragmatism, since they and their clothes will both be dry in no time in the tropical heat.

'Kampung Bahowo' consists essentially of one main road, which is actually little better than a dirt track. This heads straight from the 'main road' (although this term is used advisedly) to the beach, and is in the region of 200 metres long. From this road, just before the beach, another road of about 100 metres in length leads off at a right angle, at the end of which is Bahowo Lodge. Almost all of the village houses are situated along these two roads, although there is some 'overspill' housing across the tidal lagoon, which we call suburbia, but which is locally known as Lisum Batu.

So the people of Bahowo are poor, and wherever the 'poverty line' is drawn, Indonesian village folk are below it. It is hard, however, for us to see them in this light, since, aside from the externally conceived concept of financial poverty, the people of Bahowo lead healthy, happy and fulfilled lives. This is not African desert poverty, with the associated daily search for clean water and enough to eat; this is tropical rainforest poverty, which is a very different animal indeed.

In this regard there are two main elements that mitigate the living conditions of the village people here. Firstly, the climate, which aside from varying amounts of rainfall is constant throughout the year. The temperature, with the exception of a very few days in a year, fluctuates between 28 and 32 degrees Celsius, the rare extremes being 25 and 35 degrees. We rarely get strong winds so close to the equator, so a basic bamboo or timber shelter is really all you need.

And this is bountiful land. Below ground there is an endless and, once the well is dug, easily accessible supply of clean, fresh water. There are fish in the sea, and the rich volcanic loam together with the combination of intense tropical sunshine and reliable rain mean that there is always a ready supply of vegetables, rice and fruit. Bananas and coconuts are available everywhere, and just in the gardens of Bahowo Lodge we grow pineapples, guava, papaya and jackfruit, amongst others. So nobody ever need be hungry or reliant upon external support or donation in order to maintain a balanced and healthy diet. There is generally an 'open house' policy in the villages, and anyone needing food can normally be expected to find it in anybody else's kitchen. Nobody here need ever go sick through malnutrition, dirty water or other factors, which are so much a feature of poor communities in other parts of our world.

And they are, without doubt, the happiest people that we have ever met, unencumbered as they are by the trappings and stresses of richer societies. On occasion, if we arrive back steaming after a bad day in Manado, perhaps having been trying to unravel the deep and impenetrable mysteries of Indonesian bureaucracy, or in search of a particularly elusive item for the lodge, we can arrive at the entrance to Bahowo feeling somewhat frayed around the edges. By the time we travel the 300 metres or so to the gates of Bahowo Lodge we are in an entirely different frame of mind, having been smiled at, waved at and in general having received a greeting that would calm even the most tormented soul. Even after seven or so years, the passing of one of our cars through the village causes excitement amongst the children, and waving at the kids is a requirement of every such journey. We have often observed that if one started waving at children in England, one would probably be arrested. For the first week or so after we return to our native country we tend to behave like idiots, talking to people in lifts or queues, or striking up conversations in cafes and the like. It takes us a while to remember where we are, for the shutters to go down, and for us to become once again a part of the faceless crowd, where even fleeting eye contact is regarded with suspicion. 'You don't come from 'round here, do you?' has oft times been said to us during our period of readjustment to Western ways. And it is true, of course – we don't.

12

Of God, Death and Demons

We would like to continue this second part of our book by devoting a chapter to some religious aspects of village life in Indonesia, and giving some insight into the spiritual lives of the people of Bahowo. Bahowo village is made up of some 100 families, or around 400 souls. It is an entirely Christian village, a direct result of former Dutch rule in this part of Indonesia. The northern part of the North Sulawesi peninsula is roughly 75 per cent Christian and 20 per cent Muslim, the remaining 5 per cent being Buddhist and others.

The people hereabouts take a rather pragmatic approach to religion, and inter-faith marriages are common, in which case one of the couple will change religion. This will depend upon whichever family has the best situation for the newly married couple, which normally means the biggest house or the most money. There are a few cases of this in Bahowo village, for example Rodlan, Aris's son, married Rani, a Muslim girl from the next village, and she is now a Christian. It seems not to matter so much what you are, as long as you are something. One is made to reflect that if the rest of the world thought in this way, we would all, perhaps, be the better for it. It would at least be a start.

There are in fact two churches in Bahowo, one Protestant and one Pentecostal. This is due in large to the fact that the original founder of the village, who began life as a Protestant and who built the first Protestant church, converted to the Pentecostal church late in life, and so established and built a church of this denomination. Although it is not unusual to have two churches in a small village, even here in Bahowo it can be a socially divisive factor. At the Pentecostal church the singing and preaching is of the more enthusiastic variety that one would expect, the Protestant church being much more austere, and many of the hymns sung there on Sunday mornings are the same as those one can hear in any church in England, with Indonesian words substituted for the English ('Jerusalem' must be tricky to translate).

When we first began to make an appearance around Bahowo, there was much speculation as to which church we would attend, the assumption being that we were sure to attend one of them. When we showed only an academic interest in either, it was further assumed that we must therefore be Catholic. In the end the Pentecostal churchman could bear the suspense no longer, and rather than ask us directly, asked some friends of ours who were staying at the time which brand of Christianity we favoured. Knowing that we wished to lay the matter to rest once and for all, they told him that we worshipped the sun and the moon (for the record this was said in jest, in case anyone has just conjured up images of our carrying out pagan festivals in the coffee shop – you can't get the holly around here anyway). He hasn't spoken to us since and in fact gives us a rather wide berth. Sometimes having friends has benefits beyond the immediately obvious.

The Pentecostal church was not always where it is now, which is half way up the road out of the village and therefore some way from Bahowo Lodge. It was previously located to the front of and very close to the lodge, and we had to move it in order to create our new entrance, which we have mentioned previously. The move had definite benefits for us on a Sunday morning whilst the service was in progress. The agreement was that we would pay for the building of a new church elsewhere in the

66

village, Mr Oscar's land being decided upon by the village elders for the new location, and we agreed the sum of money for the building work. In the event Mr Oscar ended up with a nice new house, and the church was only half completed when the money ran out. We decided to regard this anomaly as a village matter.

The removal of the church also created the ideal place for us to build our swimming pool, and so at the same time as the church was being demolished, our swimming pool was being dug and constructed, the two overlapping slightly, geographically. We will leave any thoughts regarding the replacement of spirituality with Western decadence in the hands and minds of our readers.

The Protestant congregation has, almost since the time of our moving here, also been in the process of building itself a new church, although this has nothing to do with our coming. Rather it is in part due to the fact that the old church, which still exists at the time of writing, is getting rather old and shabby. It is also the case that the bigger the church, the happier everybody is, and in all Christian villages in this part of the world will be found at least one church, approximately proportionate in size with the population of the village. In any case they have adopted a different approach to building their new church. Since churches are in the normal run of things built by money donated and collected by the village folk, the building of a new church is a major and long-term commitment, spread over many years. They have therefore struck upon the rather ingenious idea of building a new church over and around the old one. In this way the old building can still be used, and once the new church is eventually completed, the old one will be demolished from the inside (bring forth the holy sledgehammer) and pulled out through the front door.

Raising the money for the new church is to a large degree left in the hands of the various committees and associations that exist in the village, and each committee or association is given a target for the amount of money it will try to raise each year. These associations include the Fishermen Association, the Fathers Association, and the Young Generation, amongst others. A few years ago the village had installed, by funds donated by the Bunaken National Marine Park, a series of boreholes, water pumps and header tanks, whereby water can now be obtained through taps, whereas previously all water had to be drawn from the village wells by a bucket and pulley system. Thus a new committee was set up, called the Water Association, although it is unclear quite what its function is. Each family in the village pays a certain sum of money each year for the upkeep and general maintenance of the pumping system, those families having a representative member within the Water Association being exempt. Their burden must be a heavy one, whatever its function, as there are twelve of them.

There is one other of note, which is the Asosiasi Orang Mati, which literally translates as the Association of People Dead, or in English parlance, The Dead People Association. This body (sorry) is not expected to raise money for the church, but to oversee the collection, safe keeping and use of collective funds for burials within the village. As a brief aside, this association came to be in a state of crisis last year, when it turned out that too many people had borrowed money from the fund, the box was empty, and that there was no money left to bury anybody. This was a 'problem big', the committee was unceremoniously replaced and a plan set up for the repayment of the borrowed money. There was a palpable unease within the village, however, lest anybody should die in the interim.

When a person dies in Bahowo, the death is announced, first by the sounding of the death bell, which is a signal for the village to act, and later by announcement by the village head. Some of the village men will take a day out from their normal labours to dig the grave, the coffin is built, and the women will prepare the body of the deceased. In the village cemetery, the position of the grave site will depend on the status of the deceased within the village, although small children will often be buried close to the family house. Such matters are organized quickly, and normally the funeral happens within 24 hours of death, a necessity given the tropical heat. There are exceptions to this, particularly if the family of the deceased must be summoned from a long distance for the funeral, in which case the body is preserved by chemical injection. This is an expensive process, however, and is avoided wherever possible. Relatives and friends of the family will visit to give their respect, the whole village will wear black for the day, and the immediate family will be expected to do so for forty days after the death.

For these forty days and nights a candle is kept alight on the grave, ostensibly to ward off the *sonkok*, of which more in a moment, but there is, of course, also biblical significance to this time period. After forty nights a wake is held, where friends and relatives of the deceased will meet, pray, and sing *masamper* songs. This is a tradition brought to coastal North Sulawesi from the island of Sangihe, which is, as we have mentioned before, the original homeland of the fishing people. One person will begin a song, and invite others to join in by touching them with a leaf or flower; the singers will then walk around 'crocodile' style. Every person is expected to know up to one hundred *masamper* songs, which are broadly divided into love songs, fishing songs and 'glory' songs. The wake begins at dusk and ends when the sun rises, which means that since Bahowo is roughly one degree north of the equator, and the day/night lengths are approximately equal all year, the wake will last for twelve hours. Locally produced palm wine once again plays a major role in events, and it is often the case that some of the singers will collapse in a drunken stupor at some time during the night; however, the singing never entirely stops until the dawn. Once the forty nights are over, this is the end of the mourning period. The wake is generally regarded as a celebration of the deceased person's life, rather than being a wholly sad affair, and afterwards the family can stop wearing black, and life for them can resume its normal pattern.

Incidentally, the good folk of Sulawesi find the idea of cremation quite abhorrent. When we told them that it is common practice for us in the West to burn our beloved ones, put the remains in a ceramic or metal vessel and place them upon the mantelpiece or elsewhere, they could not get their heads around it at all.

As we have touched upon in previous chapters, the practice of and belief in witchcraft, black magic, white magic, traditional healing methods and medicines are still very much alive in Sulawesi. These run in tandem with the much more recently introduced Christian beliefs, and the two sometimes overlap. May we now introduce you to some of the main characters, ghosts, spirits and demons that form part of the local belief system.

Probably the most feared of all is the *sonkok*. This demon is a man during the day, going about his daily business amongst his fellow villagers, and on certain nights he flies into villages in search of victims. (Female *sonkoks* are also known to exist, although less commonly, so for our purposes we will call him a man.) He particularly preys on the newly dead and newborn babies, presumably the logic behind this being that neither will offer much resistance to his evil intent. He is afraid of water, fire and red-leaved plants, and so a candle is kept alight on a newly dug grave for the forty nights of mourning, and fires are lit at night around the houses where a child has recently been born. The *sonkok* announces his arrival in a village by a call rather resembling a night bird, which goes something like 'Kok Kok Kok', from whence his name has come. The village people will not venture out of their homes if the *sonkok* is heard, but should an unwary victim be caught abroad and unawares, he or she will be carried to a local volcano and therein will be unceremoniously thrown, never to be seen again. Quite what the *sonkok* stands to gain from this *is* heinous act of evil is unclear, but I suppose that if one is a *sonkok*, it is just what one does. His favoured means of attack is to fly into the back of his victims' legs, thus knocking them to the ground. Picture, if you will, somebody sitting upright on the floor with their legs out straight in front of them and their arms to their sides. Now elevate this image to about knee-high above the ground, for this is the position that the *sonkok* will adopt in order to fly (feet first) into his victim. There have been cases reported, and which have entered village folklore, where people have fought the *sonkok* and escaped, but these are few.

The *sonkok* is a particularly clever demon, in that he is able to leave his earthly body in place during his nightly excursions, and thus, in theory at least, one could be sleeping next to one without having knowledge of the fact. (Heaven forefend, one could even be married to one.) Nevertheless, there are telltale signs that give the game away, and which the villagers will perceive. For example, somebody may be seen to be regularly having a wash in the very early morning, in an attempt, no doubt, to cleanse themselves of their nightly devilry, and the earthly manifestation of the beast will wake up feeling a bit tired. Therefore, despite their best and most devious attempts to conceal their true identity, everybody knows who the *sonkoks* are.

This raises certain questions, which doubtless will also have occurred to you. The main one that occurs to us, and that we have asked is: does he have any friends? Apparently he does, and in his earthly state is accepted as part of the village community. And then, of course, if one knows that somebody is a *sonkok*, does one make them aware of the fact, or will this tend merely to incur their wrath and therefore put one in still greater danger? One can imagine encountering a *sonkok* in an unguarded moment and saying something unfortunate, such as: 'Good morning Mr Sonkok, oops, I mean, good morning Fred.' One would not sleep well at night thereafter.

I feel that on this occasion, as with so many things relating to matters supernatural, one must cast logic to the four winds, and accept the fact that there are many mysteries that surround the *sonkok*, which shall ever remain so.

Elves also exist here, although they are more concerned with causing mischief than anything serious. In the event that one should be bothered by them, it is best to light a fire of chicken feathers, which said elves will find intensely irritating.

Ghosts and spirits are everywhere. The eldest son of Nyoman, our housekeeper, who is called Einstein, is now thirteen years old and particularly adept at perceiving the presence of the undead amongst us. Most spirits are transient by nature; however, some have taken up residence in particular places. For example, there are two children apparently residing in our coffee shop at Bahowo Lodge, and there is a very beautiful woman who haunts a certain mango tree just outside the village, and vehicles will slow and sound their horn when passing the tree so as to appease this unquiet spirit. Perhaps the most famous locally is the *hantu batu besar* or 'ghost of the big rock' on the road between Bahowo and Manado. Many people have seen this ghost, and it has been suggested as the cause of several motor accidents, although the fact that the haunted rock is situated on the brow of a steep hill and on a blind bend may also have some bearing on the matter. More locally, within Bahowo village there is a young girl who crouches down at our only road junction, at a point where, if one cuts the corner, one may very well end up falling into the storm drain that borders our village road. Said girl has very white skin and a big head, and is dressed only in a loincloth (I would quite like to see this one) and lures the unwary into said storm drain, as only a ghost can do. She did some luring last night, in fact, and caused one of our guests to fall in on his way to watch a football game at one of the village houses. Fortunately he was not hurt, although three bottles of beer that he was carrying did not survive the incident.

Before we leave the subject of death and magic, and move on to happier and more earthly matters, we would like, if we may, to briefly recount three more strange events that have occurred since we have lived in Bahowo.

The tragic case of the two sisters, and how Mr Philipus was discovered to be a vampire

There were two sisters who lived in Bahowo, both in their early twenties. On the day of the birthday of the older of the two, she was found dead in her house by her younger sister, having apparently been in good health the day before. She was duly buried, her baby was taken into care by the family, and the matter was put down as a tragic but isolated incident. It was not until Sultje, our cook, was visiting the younger sister on her birthday and found her also dead, under similar circumstances, that the village began to be convinced that there must be some magic or curse behind these deaths.

The father of Nyoman, Raymon and Tom is a well-respected white witchdoctor and traditional healer, and he was called in from his village to look into the matter, for he can perceive evil in people. He came to Bahowo, and after some searching identified Mr Philipus as being the guilty party.

Mr Philipus had something of a reputation for walking about the village on his own at night, a pastime that would immediately draw attention to him as the villagers are in general terrified of the dark, and the ghosts and spirits that dwell therein, and will never by choice walk alone at night. Nyoman's father confronted Mr Philipus and accused him of being a vampire, and told him that he must forthwith cease his evil ways and stop killing people. Mr Philipus said, okay, he would stop being a vampire, and would stop killing people. Mr Philipus still lives in the village, and the matter seems to have been laid to rest. There have been no unexplained deaths since.

Sometimes, even after several years of living in Indonesia, it is hard for us to understand.

A protection spell

One of our nearest and most active volcanoes, Gunung Mahawu, is know locally to be a place of strong magic and spirituality. Thus it was that one day thirteen young men, who considered themselves somewhat adept in matters magical, took it upon themselves to go there to practise their craft. One such spell can protect a person against physical harm (don't try this at home), and one of the thirteen volunteered to be thus protected. The spell having been cast, the others set about him with machetes, and killed him.

The now twelve men presented themselves and their deceased friend to the Manado police, who kept them in the lock-up whilst deciding what to do about this. In the end they were released after a short spell (sorry again) of detention; after all, the death was unintentional, the deceased had volunteered to be hacked with machetes, and it was in any case anybody's guess who had struck the fatal blow. The only thing the police advised was that next time they should perhaps use stronger magic, or maybe start with a penknife and see how it went from there.

Football crazy

There is often a lighter side to matters magical, as may be illustrated by the following incident, which occurred one Sunday afternoon in Bahowo.

Running a tourist lodge and taking care of the needs and wishes of our guests is something that does not stop for weekends. If we have guests we are working, and if not then we rest; either way there is little definition between the days of the week.

The only exception to this is Sunday, when the church bells announce its arrival, and the village football match occurs in the afternoon on the patch of ground designated as the football field. Socially, this is a focal point for the whole village, and having purified their souls in the morning in which ever manner has seemed fit to them, the congregations of both churches join together for the non-denominational and theologically neutral business of the afternoon soccer games.

Association football is huge in Sulawesi, and the village folk have a deep knowledge of European and world soccer. They have a far greater knowledge, for example, of the English premier league than Paula and I do, although in truth this would not be difficult, as I, at least, always preferred and played rugby union as a winter sport. (Cricket in the summer, of course, but it's best that I don't start on the subject of cricket or we will be here all day.)

Quite frequently the more energetic of our guests at Bahowo Lodge join in the Sunday afternoon football, and if we have sufficient and sufficiently sporting guests then they will form their own team. The pitch is on fairly rough but at least generally level ground, which previously also had coconut trees upon it. This fact gave the local team an advantage, since they knew by experience where the coconut trees were situated, and were thus less likely to crash into them if they were taking in the wider field of play, rather than actually watching where they were going. This at least was the case until one day one of our guests could stand no more, paid for the trees to be removed, and compensated their owner accordingly. Usually, however, the games are between teams from within the village, and inter-village football games and competitions are also common. Incidentally, the women and children also play, and the Bahowo women's team is much feared amongst the local villages.

In one such game, the Bahowo men's team was losing in the first half, and the players were complaining amongst themselves that they could not see the opposing goal, and were missing many easy scoring opportunities. (The England team could perhaps be taking notes at this stage.) There must, they surmised, be some skulduggery or magic going on, and the other team had clearly cast a missing-the-goal spell upon them. In the five-minute interval, therefore, the team retired to one of the village houses, placed a protection spell upon themselves and rubbed salt onto their legs to counter any further magic. On returning to the field of play, they threw salt at the opposing team, after which all was well, they could see the goal once more, and went on to win the game. Thus proving, perhaps, the now time-honoured adage that football is indeed a game of two halves.

And there we will leave the subject of magic, myths and monsters, and may our gods protect us from them all.

13

Love, Sex and Marriage

It has been our pleasure and privilege to be invited to many weddings since we have lived in Indonesia. These have ranged from village weddings to marriages within the upper echelons of Manadonese society. Of the two, village weddings are the best. These almost invariably involve two villages, in fact, since it is generally accepted that nobody should marry within their direct community. This in turn is because certain families tend to dominate within the individual villages, and thus there is a fairly good chance that two young people from the same village will be related to each other, however distantly.

The religious and social context within which the young village people grow up does not allow for any thought of sex before marriage. In fact, particularly in the Pentecostal church, it seems, they are threatened with fire, brimstone and eternal damnation if they stray from the path, so to speak. And so of course they do not. Except of course they do, and so on many occasions the blushing bride is showing a slight bump in the abdominal region on the happiest day of her life. The young man, should he decide to do the decent thing, which he almost invariably does, will normally be accepted into the girl's family and all sins of the flesh will eventually be forgiven. If he does not do the decent thing, his next option is to run away and live in the forest. We have witnessed both of these possible scenarios, and the forests hereabouts are full of people who have run away, for many reasons.

In Indonesia, girls come of age at seventeen years old, and at that age can legally have sex and marry, although one does not necessarily follow from the other. If a boy or man is found to have had sex with an underage girl, then he will almost certainly go to prison. If an unfortunate accident occurs below this age and the girl becomes pregnant, she or her family will often forge her birth papers to bring her in line with the law, and thus allow her to marry. This may be all very well, but if the couple subsequently have problems in the relationship, then the boy or man can get into serious trouble at any time later for marrying a girl illegally. She thus will forever have a hold over him.

Once a girl is married, there is a perfectly well-established system of birth control and family planning, which in Bahowo is administered by Martha, our village nurse, of whom we will hear later. This service is not free, but it is, at least, readily available, thus a family can and will often wait five or more years before having a second child, and most families in Bahowo have only two children. The problem is that this service is not available to young, unmarried girls, and the social and religious stigma attached to sex before marriage is such that young people would not in any case take advantage of the possibility if it existed. The girl will be asked to produce a husband before she is issued with any precautionary devices or chemicals. On public display in the Bahowo clinic there is a very neatly drawn plan of the village showing the individual houses, with colour-coded drawing pins stuck into each house. Red pins mean that there is a pregnant woman in residence, silver pins mean a young baby, and gold pins indicate that somebody in the house is taking contraception. One might say, therefore, that patient confidentiality is not high on the list of priorities.

So it is that, whereas in Western and more 'liberal' societies, where it is possible to have a number of sexual partners without long-term consequence before becoming more deeply involved with any one person, in the circumstances prevailing in rural Indonesia it is very common for young people to have to marry their first sexual partner, and at a young age. At weddings here the happy couple will tend to look rather bewildered by the whole experience, and can often hardly be said to 'know' each other at all, except in the biblical sense. Love, in the deep way that we understand it in the West, is a rare beast.

At a wedding the priest may well (and often does) orate with great enthusiasm regarding the sanctity of marriage and the sinfulness of intimacy without it, in an attempt to shut the stable door. Unfortunately, the horse has often already bolted.

For all that, weddings are always happy affairs, and a good excuse for a village banquet of sumptuous and delicious Indonesian food. The women, normally about ten or more in number, spend two days and nights preparing the feast, whilst the men erect a temporary bamboo and canvas shelter in the garden of either the bride's or the groom's parents. Organizing such a banquet is an expensive business, and many families will donate food, perhaps in the form of a pig or sack of rice, the favour being returned when a wedding occurs in the family of those giving the food.

Providing the remainder of the paraphernalia required for a wedding, such as invitations, bridesmaids' dresses and of course the wedding dress itself, is a thriving business, the numerous salons being almost exclusively run by 'ladyboys' who are always very much in evidence during the reception, and of whom more is written in due course.

On the day itself, the church service is held in the morning, from whence the married couple and their attendants will process to the reception. There are commonly five or six bridesmaids and always the same number of male ushers, and these are expected to pair up for the occasion.

The reception itself is formatted differently from marriages in the West, in that the speeches are always given first, before the food is laid out and eaten. The logic of this, we have been told, is that once they have eaten, people will tend to drift off and avoid the speeches, thus depriving the speakers of their moment of oratory glory. This is perhaps understandable since, once an Indonesian has gained possession of a microphone it is the devil's own job to wrest it from their grasp. Thus do the speeches tend to go on long after the speaker has lost the attention of the audience, and there are usually four or five such speeches. There is always a speech from the priest (fire and brimstone), usually Mr Benjamin (the village head), the bride's father, the groom's father, visiting relatives and others. By the time the final prayer is over and the order to eat is given, the wedding guests are either asleep or in a state of high agitation, and always very hungry. The promise of eventual food also draws the attention of many of the village dogs, pigs and chickens, and throughout the speeches and reception in general there is much coming and going of domestic animals, and dog fights will often break out, which seems to do little to dampen the oratory zeal of the speaker, but does at least provide some distraction for the human element in the congregation.

We are normally given place of honour at such events. Frankly, we would rather blend into the background, but such seems to be our social duty. We normally have our own table of food, which may include Western delicacies denied to the other guests, such as chips. The cooking of chips, which before our arrival in the village were an unknown phenomenon, started when they were requested by guests of Bahowo Lodge, missing perhaps their culinary home comforts, and so we taught Sultje how to cook them. She subsequently and proudly presented them at a wedding feast, exclusively for our delectation, and so now at every wedding, despite our preference for the local food, it is expected that we eat chips.

The final event before eating is the ritual giving and feeding of cake between the two families. The bride will feed cake to the groom's mother and father, the groom will do likewise to the bride's parents, then the respective parents will feed each other and finally the bride and groom. Official wedding documents will have already been signed by this time, but it is the feeding of the cake that ritually seals the marriage, rather as we would exchange rings.

Only once did we see this go wrong, when a Swiss friend of ours was marrying an Indonesian, and her mother, being unsure of this ritual, ate the cake herself when she should have fed it to the groom's parents. (She was probably very hungry.) Another piece of cake was provided and the ceremony continued without further mishap.

During village weddings, once the eating has begun the event relaxes and everybody has a jolly good time. This will continue until, at a certain point, all of the guests must shake the hand of the bride, groom and their now in-laws, and the reception is officially over. Usually at village weddings the families will have hired a speaker system that would not embarrass the Albert Hall, which is placed in the front garden, and the whole village will benefit from the sounds which emanate there from. The dancing will always continue into the wee hours of the morning, and often until dawn.

Enjoyable as they are, there can always be too much of a good thing, and on one particular Sunday a couple of years ago we had no less than six village weddings in Bahowo on the same day. This involved six separate speaker systems, two of which were set up in adjacent gardens, and the cacophony of noise throughout the village was enough to raise the dead from their slumbers, or summon forth the four horsemen of the apocalypse. We were also left with the politically sensitive decision as to which wedding reception we should attend, a decision made easier by the fact that Mr Benjamin's daughter was one of the girls getting married, and everybody would understand that we should attend the reception given by the village headman. Nevertheless, it would have been socially irresponsible of us not to at least pay a brief visit to some of the other weddings; it is rude not to eat at least something, and I doubt if we have eaten so much food in one day before or since.

'Society' weddings, in which the great and good of Manado get spliced, will follow much the same format as village weddings, only with more pomp and circumstance, and the speeches tend to be even longer. They are held in especially designated banqueting halls, one of which happens to be above a supermarket. One therefore is forced to witness and be a part of the somewhat bizarre spectacle of people dressed in their wedding finery going through the same checkout channel as those other people doing the weekly shop.

Such weddings are bought as a 'package', including beautiful Indonesian girls who act as usherettes, and there is a stage on which the ceremonial aspects will take place and group photographs will be taken. This photographic session can delay the food by a further hour or more, and since we are almost always the only Western people on the guest list, we are always required to be in the wedding photos.

Another essential difference between these events and village weddings soon becomes apparent, for at society weddings there is never enough food. Everybody knows this, and when the order to eat is finally given the congregation moves as one fluid body to the buffet tables. Normally civilized people (bearing in mind that this is the cream of Manado society) behave like wild beasts to the kill, social etiquette is abandoned in the mad scramble for the fish curry, corruption is rife, as serving spoons are passed between family members and those currying (once again, sorry) favour. ('Remember I passed you the serving spoon at X's wedding, you owe me…') Life-long bonds of friendship are made or broken over the fried rice, and we have seen a spit-roasted pig stripped to the bone at a rate that would embarrass a shoal of ravenous piranha fish. We quickly learned that we cannot compete in such a scrimmage, have accepted the fact that we will not be fed, and so have adopted the policy of either eating before we arrive or stopping off at a café in town on the way home.

Whichever form the wedding takes, the bride and groom take little part in the proceedings of the reception. They are expected

82

to sit in adjacent chairs on a raised platform or stage and watch proceedings, rising only for the cake feeding ritual. That said, the bride will often change her meringue-style dress up to six times during the evening. She may start off in blue, and an hour later will have changed into yellow, and so on, which can be quite disconcerting for the ladies present. The men present will probably not have noticed.

The term *bulan madu*, or honeymoon, is used here to describe the few days just after the marriage, which for village couples is not marked by any particular change in their daily routine. Indonesians living in the provinces rarely have passports, village people never, and the folk of Bahowo hardly ever travel further than Manado. In any event there will never be enough money left over after the expense of the wedding itself for the couple to indulge in any leisure activities.

And so, the day after the wedding feast, the men take down the bamboo and canvas awning, everything borrowed is returned to its respective owner, and the young couple settle down to the trials and tribulations of married life with the in-laws, and await the arrival of a third family member, usually somewhat less than nine months hence.

Most weddings occur between a man and woman of the same faith, and we have mentioned that inter-faith marriages are not uncommon. Our next story, however, falls somewhere between the two, as you will see.

Islam and Christianity, as they relate to Mr Willy's teeth

Willy lives in Bahowo village, his house bordering onto our land. He is about thirty years old, and has a very nice, older wife and a young daughter. Despite this he took it upon himself (or perhaps, as is the way with these things, he had no choice in the matter) to have an emotional entanglement with a Muslim girl from

Manado, to the point where, as it later transpired, he was leading something of a double life. In Bahowo he was Willy, in Manado he was Wally. His entanglement became such, and he became so embroiled with said girl that he agreed to marry her. Now, it is a fact that under Indonesian state law, if you are of Christian faith and already have one wife, you cannot have another one, at least not at the same time. Willy figured out, however, that despite his existing wife being a Christian, his soon-to-be wife was a Muslim, so that would be all right, as Muslims are allowed up to four wives. All he had to do was to become a Muslim and all his troubles would be over.

Thus it was that one day he engineered an argument with his wife and told her he was leaving her, having previously cunningly arranged that his brother should pick him up on his motorbike, and he set off on his wedding day to begin his new life as a Muslim. They had not gone more than a few hundred metres on the journey, however, when they had a road accident, in the course of which Willy fell off said motorbike and knocked his front teeth out.

His eligibility for marriage had thus been compromised and somewhat diminished, and in any case he ended up in hospital, fortunately not seriously hurt but certainly the element of surprise, which had been one key factor in his favour, had been removed, and the wedding ceremony had to be called off. Having failed to appear for his intended betrothal, word reached his wife-to-be (or as it happened, not-to-be) of his unfortunate circumstances, and she attempted to visit him in the hospital. Meantime his actual wife got wind of the situation, she also came to the hospital, and there the stark truth of Willy's dastardly plan was revealed to them both. His real wife staked her claim of existing owner-ship, and so the bride-to-be left without further dispute, perhaps to ponder upon the ways of men, be they Christian or other-wise. Thus it was that Willy had to return to Bahowo, having fewer wives than he had intended, and fewer teeth than he had left with.

Dentistry in Manado is expensive for village people, and they avoid it wherever possible. Willy attempted to overcome this problem by inserting a piece of wood between his good teeth. This proved less than successful, and so after a few months of saving his money he had enough to have a plate of false teeth installed. All would have been well, were it not for the fact that Willy has something of a drinking habit, and from time to time when he loses control of the situation, he also loses control of his teeth, and they fall out somewhere about the village. So it is that sometimes an announcement is made over the village public address system that, if anybody has found Willy's' teeth, could they please return them to him. So Willy still lives amongst us, and is to this day, a Christian. Allah be praised.

14

Morals, Mores and Dressing Up

In Indonesia, or at least in Manado, 'ladyboys' are men who dress as women, and tend to emphasize their femininity by adopting feminine mannerisms such as flicking the hair and so on, which of course women do not actually do. These are distinct from 'banshees', who are gay men who do not dress as women. Both are rather regarded as a curiosity by the heterosexual community, and there is generally no feeling of animosity or aggression toward them. We have never heard the local Christian church voice opinion or take any moral stand on the issue of homosexuality, and although we have less experience as regards the Muslim community, we imagine that the generally mild and accepting nature of the people hereabouts would override any religious intolerance.

Given that Indonesia as a whole is a predominantly Muslim country, the dress code is fairly liberal in and around Manado, and it is perfectly acceptable for girls to wear tight jeans, short skirts, high heels, and so on. Muslim girls and women wear the *kerudung*, which is equivalent to the hijab, but their faces are not covered. Public displays of affection between men and women are, however, rare, and recently an act was put before the Indonesian parliament that would have made it illegal for men and women to kiss in public under the laws of 'pornography'. The act was not passed, and never became law, but it demonstrates the fact that extremist factions operate within government. On the other hand (there I go again), it is not uncommon on the streets of Manado to see heterosexual men holding hands with other heterosexual men, or women holding hands with women, as a sign of friendship. Homosexual men holding hands would not, however, be considered morally acceptable.

All of this is probably the consequence of Manado being a predominantly Christian city, against the backdrop of the mainly Muslim central government in Jakarta, which makes all the rules. A generally less liberal attitude to sexual matters manifests itself in the censorship laws that exist in Indonesia as a whole. For example, there is absolutely no sex shown on Indonesian television, and films bought from mainstream Indonesian stores are always heavily censored for sexual content. Not so for violence, however, and it is perfectly fine to show scenes of the most gruesome and gratuitous violence, genocide and murder, as long as nobody kisses anybody else.

'Pirate' copies of films are sold illegally but quite openly by stalls in downtown Manado. Occasionally these are raided by the police, and unless the correct amount of money changes hands they go underground for periods of time, and their customers have to buy films in darkened rooms. Before long, however, the stallholders re-emerge onto the streets and business resumes its normal course. These films are not censored; however, in order to watch uncensored films ourselves we bring them from England. From time to time we watch these imported films in the evenings with our Indonesian friends, and all is well so long as no intimacy is shown between men and women, as this causes them acute embarrassment, and they hide their faces.

Given all of this, there is often an unconscious departure from the locally held morals, caused by the village people not understanding English and yet buying and wearing imported or copied foreign goods. I well remember on one of our first visits to Bahowo one of the village girls proudly showing us a cassette tape that she had bought. 'I like to dance!' she announced with great enthusiasm. The cassette had English song titles, and they were the most obscene that we had ever had the misfortune to come across. The poor girl clearly had not the least idea of the lyrical content of the music to which she was dancing. This phenomenon is particularly apparent when it comes to slogans written in English on T-shirts. At a village wedding recently, one of the ladies who was serving the food at the buffet table, and who we know to be a pious and religious person of high moral standing, was sporting a T-shirt bearing the slogan 'Knock me off' in large letters. We did not enlighten her.

15

Unholy Water

There are no natural lakes or other significant standing water in the coastal areas of North Sulawesi, the only lake of any size in this part of the peninsula being Lake Tondano, which is in the highlands. So, if you need to find fresh water in the coastal villages such as Bahowo, you must dig. Our village is situated above a huge underground reservoir, and wherever you dig, you will eventually find water. In certain low-lying parts of the village the water is only 3 or 4 metres below ground level, at Bahowo Lodge, being in a more elevated position, we have to dig to 10 or 12 metres. The fact that there is plentiful water here is in large part responsible for the village remaining and growing, as the presence of water is by no means guaranteed everywhere. We know of a certain pioneering Belgian gentleman who bought land further along the peninsula, hired the required drilling equipment and spent weeks searching unsuccessfully for water, and had to abandon his venture.

We have three wells in the grounds of Bahowo Lodge. The first, which was here before our arrival, was formerly used by the Pentecostal church, and now serves our swimming pool and gardens. The second, which provides water for the lodge itself, was dug during construction of the building, and so we were not here to witness the process. The third, built during our tenure, is located some 200 metres from the lodge, and was ostensibly dug to serve a Minahasa-style house, which we have built for a friend.

We gave the village the option of whether we employ the services of an industrial drill to dig a narrow borehole, a process that would have taken about a day, or whether the village would prefer to dig the well by hand. They chose the latter, since it would provide several weeks' work for three men. The cost to us was to be roughly the same either way, and we were in no hurry, so on the appointed day, Abner, Isaac and Michael began digging. Incidentally, Isaac was formerly Ishmael, before he married a Christian girl in Bahowo and changed his religion and so his name, another example of cross-pollination between the religions.

The first couple of metres were easy, topsoil and subsoil, and then, as expected, we hit the coral. These are ancient coral beds, which have become crystallized and are thus very hard. The upper coral is some 10 to 12 metres above current sea level, and the villagers believe that this is because God took the water from the sea and used it to make the rivers and lakes. We rather prefer the idea that it is as a result either of the natural lowering of sea levels during past ice ages, or uplifting of the land, or some combination thereof. In any event, this coral layer continued down for about 10 metres, until finally we hit upon the bedrock, in which the water is found.

This digging process was carried out entirely by hand, using hammers and chisels. A length of bamboo was suspended on supports above the hole, and the excavated material brought up by means of a rope and pulley system, in buckets. At any one time, one man would be in the hole and the other two at the surface, and towards the end, conditions at the bottom of the hole were so hot, dark and airless that we had to run a cable down to a lamp and electric fan, in order to make working possible. Even so, 20 minutes was about as long as one man could stay there. There was great joy when finally we hit the damp bedrock, and a further metre of digging through this (which in itself was no easy task) created a reservoir of clear, open water. The digging process took some eight weeks.

There then followed the perhaps even more precarious operation of lining the well with concrete rings, which, being about 900 mm in diameter, are rather heavy. These were swung out onto the bamboo pole on a rope, and then lowered into the well. One man would stand inside the well, on the preceding ring, and position the new ring onto the ring on which he was standing, all done, of course, wearing the regulation safety flip-flops. We were very pleased when this process was finished without incident. The outside of the rings was then in-filled with previously excavated soil, the well-head was finished off with a traditional palm roof, and so we created another permanent source of clean, pure groundwater.

Last year, parts of North Sulawesi suffered a drought lasting some five months. Forest fires abounded, people lost their entire crops of cloves, nutmeg, bananas and so on, the levels of Lake Tondano dropped to unprecedented levels, and people in villages not far from here had to buy in water. The wells in Bahowo village continued to give water throughout, something that we and our guests at the lodge were very thankful for, and we were all greatly relieved when the rains finally came.

16

What's in a Name?

Especially in the early days of Bahowo Lodge, when we and our staff would be speaking different languages, in order to lessen the problems of communication and nomenclature between the staff and management, we had a tendency sometimes to avoid using names when talking about village people and others. We would tend rather to use whatever noun or verb would most easily identify the particular person in question. For example, one man in the village once, several years ago, planted about two hundred pineapple plants in our garden. Thereafter he has been known as 'Mr Pineapple', or, in fact 'Mr Nanas', which is the Indonesian version.

We buy our fish at Bahowo Lodge directly from the village fishermen, who fish, usually at night, from the small one-man *londes*, or fishing boats, that are used here. These are narrow, canoe-style boats with outlying bamboo-pole stabilizers. Traditionally, these would have been paddled, but nowadays they often have small, outboard motors. Anyone who has had a successful day or night's fishing, which will usually consist of one or two fishes, will bring the catch to the lodge. Thus we and our guests benefit from delicious, freshly caught fish, and the fish-erman will avoid a journey to the market. 'Mr Fish' would be responsible for catching most of the fish supplied to the Lodge, and 'Mrs Fish' would deliver it. This system worked well until a second 'Mr Fish', and hence a second 'Mrs Fish', became regular suppliers. We had to make a distinction between the two, and so the first Mrs Fish became 'Mrs Fish No Signal' (she is hard of hearing) and the second Mrs Fish became 'Mrs Fish Blah Blah Blah', as she has a tendency to talk rather a lot. This, of course, has rather the reverse effect of simplifying or shortening a given name, but the system has stuck. Thus if we have a problem with our plumbing at the lodge, we must call 'Mr Water' (formerly 'Mr Toilet', but we decided that this was somewhat demeaning), and 'Mr Listrik' (electricity) deals with all matters electrical. Other examples include: 'Mr Churchman' the vicar, 'Mr Mini-shop' the local shopkeeper, 'Mrs Itchy', who is so called because she is looking for a new husband, 'Mr Cups and Saucers' (of whom more later) and 'Mr Choppy-Choppy', who some years ago hacked his father to death with a machete.

As a brief aside, we asked why, therefore, was Mr Choppy-Choppy still at liberty, and it was explained to us that his father had treated both him and his mother very badly, and that he (Mr Choppy-Choppy) had been provoked into this extreme measure. The wife of the deceased raised no complaint in the matter, and so the police let him off on the grounds of provocation.

'Johnny Chainsaw' (having a rather more conventional form of nickname) is thus called to distinguish him from 'Johnny the Builder Johnny'. Johnny Chainsaw does not live in Bahowo any more. A couple of years ago he and his chainsaw were lopping down a coconut tree outside the village, and in so doing, by dint of the fact that he did not have complete control over the direction in which the tree would fall, brought down the power lines. Three days without power to the local villages including Bahowo ensued, whilst the electricity company sought recompense for the unfortunate incident. Far from obtaining said compensation, they did not even obtain Johnny Chainsaw, who had run to the forest (where he would have found the company of young men who had sown their wild oats a little too successfully, and other fugitives from society), never to return. Just as an aside, it occurs whilst writing this that it is a most unfortunate and difficult thing to try to remain hidden and inconspicuous when your livelihood depends on using a chainsaw, which can be heard echoing around the still, tropical air for miles around. Anyway, we digress from our given subject of names.

Anybody who has ever tried to name a cow, or indeed cows, will appreciate the difficulties inherent therein. But I am jumping ahead, and should tell the story from the beginning.

Mr Phillips (AKA Mr Cow – you may by now have noticed that this is not rocket science) is a cow man. Cows are used in rural Indonesia as beasts of burden, to pull the carts, or *rodas*, that transport rice across the paddies and coconuts or other produce from the plantations to the processing sites or to market, often across very rough terrain. They are not eaten, being too valuable as working animals, and beef does not constitute part of the diet in rural Indonesia. In former times, Mr Phillips had a working team of cows, and was thus able to fulfil his role. At a certain point, some years before our arrival in Bahowo, the villagers had a land dispute with some Chinese people and needed to raise money to fight their cause. In order to do so they sold off the Bahowo cows and, although the land claim was successful, this left Bahowo without its much needed cows and cart.

This was a 'problem big', and on hearing of these difficulties we resolved to put matters to rights at the first opportunity. There is a certain girls' school in Berkshire, England, called Queen Anne's School, whose pupils have done wonderful work over the years in raising money for the social needs of Bahowo village. We will be writing of this in greater depth in a subsequent chapter, but suffice for now to say that the girls agreed to our proposal that some of the donated money could be used to buy two cows for the village. We also have a very dear friend in England, Janet Fookes, whom I met initially in my former life as a landscape gardener when I was commissioned to build the extensive gardens of her house in East Sussex. She is also variously known as Lady Fookes, Dame Janet, and The Baroness Fookes of Plymouth. She is a keen lover of animals, and has been from the outset a tremendous help to us in our fundraising efforts for Bahowo. In any case, she also expressed a willingness to help us to buy cows for Bahowo, so now we had the possibility of buying four cows, or two working teams.

In order to buy cows in this part of North Sulawesi, it is advisable to buy direct from the cow market in the Minahasa highland region. Thus it was that I found myself, early one morning and with our friend the Baroness, and of course Mr Phillips, the cow man, in the cow market in Tomohon. We (the Baroness and I) had never bought cows before, and spent the time walking knowledgably around, pulling ears and considering and discussing the finer points of the cows that were up for sale, whilst Mr Phillips set about the actual task in hand of selecting cows of the right age and condition for our requirements.

Eventually, having spent a thoroughly enjoyable few hours at the market, we agreed upon the young calves that we should buy, the price was set, and we returned rather triumphantly to Bahowo with a certificate of sale and some new cows for the village.

This left us, to bring us back to where we began this story, with only one decision, namely what we should call them. Now, it should be said at this juncture that the villagers thought us rather eccentric to want to give them names at all; they were, after all, only cows, however important they would be to the village economy. However, certain conventions must be adhered to in such matters. Since one of our village school teachers is called Daisy, that possibility was ruled out, and Buttercup just doesn't fit right in Indonesia (they don't have them here). In the end we decided to place this responsibility in the hands of our friend the Baroness, who would name two of them, and the younger children of Bahowo Primary School, who would come up with a list of possible names for the others, from which the girls of Queen Anne's school would make the final decision.

The boys came up with names such as (and here we will trans-late from the original Indonesian) Pig, Horse, Tiger, Crocodile and Cow. The girls got the hang of it rather better, and their selected names included Sunshine, Flower, Babe and Rose.

So in the end we had Mata Hari (which means sunshine), Babe, Rose and Snowdrop; they are now doing great work for the people of Bahowo, and Mr Phillips is a cow man once more.

Another naming incident occurred out of the blue one day when one of the village girls, Rachel, who was heavily pregnant but not yet due to give birth, came up to the lodge and announced to one of our staff that she had abdominal pains and please could we take her to the doctor in one of our cars. We decided that Aris, who was driving for us at the time, would drop her off on the way to town, since he was going that way to buy some beer for the lodge. An hour or so later, after he had finished loading the crates, they set off, and had not been gone for more than a few minutes when Rachel went into premature labour. There then ensued a high-speed journey through town to the hospital, with Rachel screaming in pain and Aris screaming for clear passage through the heavy traffic. She gave birth to a healthy baby within minutes of arriving at the hospital, the birth having been without further complication. The baby was a girl and, as a token of thanks for our help, Rachel named her child 'Paula Kecil', or 'Little Paula', as it translates. Had it been a boy, it would have been 'Little Phil'.

It is usually the custom in Bahowo and amongst the Sangihe people in general that the parents do not name their own chil-dren, but rather that the child is named by a family member or godparent. We have twice been asked to name children in the village; the first grandson of Aris is thus called Tristan (we must have been feeling classically operatic at the time), and the second son of Nyoman, who is our godson, is called Sebastian. This happened more by chance than design, as on the morning of Sebastian's birth I was sitting drinking coffee with Aris, and we were discussing names for children. At that time Aris was still high up in the hierarchy of the village, and so, as it later transpired, it fell upon him to ask me what I thought would be a good name for the newly born child. I came up with the name Sebastian, and Aris immediately went to Melda, the mother, to tell her that this is what the child shall be called. Fortunately, she liked the name.

Nowadays it is fashionable in the villages to name children after famous footballers or film stars. Thus we have Renaldo, Gerard, Leonardo DiCaprio (we kid you not) and others. Einstein was so named by his grandfather because Einstein was a clever man (although this could be something of an understatement) and he hoped that some of it would rub off. We may think of it as an unusual name, but everything is relative, I suppose. There is also the custom in the villages of giving children within a family almost the same name. For example, the lovely identical twin girls who are daughters of Yohanis the bus driver are called Stefi and Stefa, and in one family the second eldest boy is called Walter, pronounced as in 'wall', the third eldest son is also called Walter, although his name is pronounced as in 'tally', the fourth eldest is Walder ('tally' again) and the only daughter is Waltje (pronounced waltchay). The eldest son is called Abraham.

Amongst the Sangihe people it is also the custom not to call people in everyday parlance by their given name, but rather by their respective and relative position within the siblings of the family. Thus the eldest son is always called 'Kaka' (the 'a' being as in 'cat'), the second born son 'Yaya' (the 'a' as in 'car'), the third 'Arah' (cat), the fourth Ari (cat), the fifth Bu (Boo), the sixth 'Paada' ('car') and the seventh Uto (Ooto). Girls, respectively from one to five (and please always sound the first 'a' twice, as in Ma-akang,), are Maakang (cat), Maarah (car), Maari (car), Maadeh (car) and Mabu (cat).

The people of Minahasa, of course, have their own no less valid traditions, although we know less about these as we have less day-to-day contact with them. Since we are on the subject of names, however, we can at least tell you that the folk of the various tribes of Minahasa believe that the first man and woman to live on the earth, and from which all of the tribes have descended, were called Toar and Lumimuut, would you Adam and Eve it.

And finally, if you wish to insult a woman locally, call her 'Basket eyes'. This apparently means that she is 'looking at men' in a certain way, which is not regarded as a good thing to be doing. We don't quite understand this either, and the worst thing you can call a man hereabouts is a 'Crocodile boy'. Let us move on.

17

A Village Fete and How Mr Cups and Saucers Got His Name

Each year, on 17th August, Indonesia celebrates the end of Dutch colonial rule, and Independence Day, or 'freedom day', events are a national phenomenon. It is a public holiday, and the villages and towns are adorned with red and white bunting, these being the colours of the Indonesian flag.

It so happened that one year we had two of the girls from Queen Anne's school, Georgia and Fari (the 'a' is pronounced as in 'cat'), staying at the lodge, as part of our mutual attempts to cement ties between the school and Bahowo village. We were one day discussing ways in which cultural gaps could be bridged, and in the course of our discussions came up with the idea of holding an English-style event in the village school, which would include sack races, egg and spoon races and so on. This we duly did, and it was a huge success, none of the children having engaged in such activities before. However, it being a school event, the village populous in general was not involved, except as spectators, and our staff proposed that we should hold a similar but larger event for the entire village, to be held on the village football field on Independence Day. We agreed somewhat tentatively that it could be a good idea, the only alternative that year being for the village to attend a volleyball match in the next village, and we duly set about the organization. The day would include a coconut shy, apple-bobbing, various races including egg and spoon, sack and three-legged, a free raffle, refreshments and of course a village tug of war.

Much preparation followed, and we had certain misgivings, not knowing how the good folk of Bahowo would react on a village scale to such a very English event. Our misgivings were heightened, rather, by the fact that the preceding two or three weeks saw an unseasonable amount of rain, and we had tropical downpours every day, which in a way made it feel even more English.

In any event, we were undeterred, and rice sacks, rope and all the required paraphernalia were assembled, as well as several hundred small prizes, and of course the raffle prizes. These, we thought, should be of a practical rather than frivolous nature, and of the kind that the villagers would not buy for themselves. In the end they were to be a bedding and sheet set as first prize, second prize was a ceramic tea set, and third prize was an electric iron.

And so the day itself dawned, and the villagers eyed proceedings with some suspicion as we set out the running track, placed coconuts atop bamboo sticks, and filled a large plastic tub with water into which we then placed apples. (They probably thought that the silly English had finally lost it.)

Since we still considered the day to be ostensibly for the village children, we rounded some up, or rather dragged them from their homes, and brought them forth into the arena. To the first three or four children, we said, 'Put your hands behind your back, immerse your heads in this tub of water and try to get an apple out with your teeth.' This took some time to produce results, as it is not an easy task for small mouths, but finally one child got the hang of it, and emerged soaking wet but victorious, with an apple firmly clenched in his jaws. Indonesian village children are very polite, and he thanked us and placed the apple back in the water. We told him that he could keep the apple. Apples are an expensive, imported fruit in Indonesia, and rarely if ever eaten by village people, so this gave an entirely new dimension to the situation, and as a small rock will start an avalanche, very soon other children assembled around the water tub, and before long there was not enough head room within said tub to accommodate all of the contestants without danger of mass concussion. Order had to be brought upon proceedings, and the Young Generation Association stepped in with notepad and paper to put matters to rights. The names of the contestants were carefully written down before each bout, and the winner's name duly noted. Before long everybody wanted a go, and the children were muscled aside by their mothers, who with grim determination set about the task of securing an apple. We would ask you to try to visualize the scene: five or six village women with their heads in a tub of water, with by now most of the rest of the village assembled around the tub, the noise of excited screaming building to a crescendo with each bout.

The village men preferred the coconut shy, where we were offering cigarettes to anyone who could knock the coconut off the bamboo pole with a tennis ball from ten paces; three balls per contestant, one cigarette per successful throw. Before long people were attempting to throw plastic balls into a jar, or to eat doughnuts that had been suspended along a piece of string, using only their mouths, and meanwhile the apple tub continued to draw the crowds.

By now we had the attention of the whole village, and decided to begin the races. The children quickly learned how to cover 20 metres or so inside a rice sack, or two of them would attempt to do so with their legs tied to each other; meanwhile the onlookers dissolved in fits of uncontrolled laughter. We thought these events would be for the children only. How wrong could we have been. Before long the vicar was making good ground against Mr Minishop in the sack race, with Mr Choppy-Choppy coming up strong

105

on the outside. To our great surprise even the head of the Pentecostal church, normally the most austere and serious of individuals, joined in the egg and spoon race.

And so the day proceeded, and throughout, the Young Generation Association continued to keep their meticulous records in preparation for the prize-giving ceremony, which we decided should be held at the end of the day. Raymon took over the microphone and took on the job as master of ceremonies and commentator, announcing each race as it began with the names of the contestants. Free tickets for the grand prize draw were given out, with a maximum of one to each family.

After a few hours we decided that refreshments would be in order, and the village women provided tea and home-made dough-nuts for everybody, they having been asked to spend the previous evening making about four hundred doughnuts, for reasons that were unclear to them at the time. There was a general lull in proceedings as everyone tucked in, and we thought perhaps that the general mayhem would begin to subside somewhat. Once again we were proved to be wrong, and the contests began anew, in fact with renewed vigour, the contestants being suitably refreshed and ready to face the challenges of the afternoon.

Another person to benefit from the event was the ice cream seller, who quite by chance turned up at an opportune time on his motorbike and ice cream dispenser. We limited the ice creams to children only, but nevertheless bought over ninety of them. We suspected that a certain amount of doubling back to rejoin the end of the queue was going on, so Melda was sent to police matters and make sure that no further skulduggery occurred.

By late afternoon we felt that we had to intervene, as with only a couple of hours of daylight remaining, and no sign of any let-up in the races, we had not yet held the tug of war, given out the prizes or held the raffle.

So in due process we came to the prize-giving, whereby all victorious adult participants were given shampoo, soap or coffee sachets, perfume sticks and costume jewels for the girls, hair gel for the boys, and so on. In the event we made sure that nobody who had participated in the day's activities left without a prize or gift.

Finally it came to the grand prize draw, and the numbers were pulled out of the hat and announced with some ceremony. The vicar won first prize with the bedding set, and ironically our then clothes-washer, Sultje, won the iron, one of which, of course, she already had. It was the winning of the second prize, however, that caused the most general enjoyment, as a certain gentleman whose actual name has never been known to us was in such a state of high excitement at winning the tea set, that he has forever since been known to us and our staff as Mr Cups and Saucers.

And so ended the day, which, as it turned out, had been dry and sunny throughout, and we returned to our homes, the villagers not quite knowing what they had experienced, we feeling that we had perhaps taken a small step forward in bringing together two very different cultures, and done our part, at least for a day, in making the world a smaller and happier place.

What we did not expect, and had certainly not anticipated at the outset, was that the next year on Independence Day the village elders asked that we do it again, and so the English fete has become an annual event in a small fishing village, far away.

18

Families, Fireworks and Festivals

Indonesia is predominantly a Muslim country, being the most fundamental to the west, becoming more moderate the further east one looks on the atlas, blending into the mainly Protestant but sometimes Catholic Christian areas to the extreme east of the archipelago. The only oddity is Bali, which has by dint of some historical influence become mainly Hindu, adopting and adapting Indian traditions such as the ubiquitous Dragon Dance, which is performed for tourists on a daily basis.

Sulawesi is somewhere at the meeting point between Islam and Christianity, and so, in common one supposes with most of Indonesia, we have 'red days' on the calendar to allow the celebration of all Muslim and Christian festivals. Red days are something like bank holidays in Europe; schools and government offices are closed, and the general populous has a day or days off. In Bahowo, as one would expect, Christmas is the main focal point of the year in terms of celebration. The families here save money throughout the year for their annual crate of Coca-Cola, and the children drink chocolate milk on Christmas morning, it being the only day of the year when they are allowed, for financial reasons, to drink milk in any form. The fatted pigs are slaughtered, and it is a time for disparate and far-flung families to get together to mend old feuds and begin new ones.

Families and family ties are extremely important, in fact one might say of paramount importance, in rural Indonesia. In the West, it is of course now often possible for those of us with the time and necessary computer literacy to trace our family and ancestry by technological means. In the normal run of things, however, by comparison to Indonesian village folk, we have lost track of it completely. From time to time we get mail at the lodge via Facebook from people with whom one of us shares a common surname (neither of which are, in fact, common surnames), and we have not the least idea who they are, or how we may be related to them. In Indonesian villages, everybody knows who is related to whom, and by what means, often in a mind-numbingly complex set of interrelations. We have, or perhaps I should say that Paula has, a basic grasp of who in Bahowo is married to whom, which child belongs to which family, how they in turn relate to others in the village, and so on. Take this outside the village boundaries and it becomes ever more bewildering, and yet everybody here knows, for example, who their distant cousins are, no matter how many times removed they may be. At Christmas they crash together in great numbers.

In the villages there is always a morning church service on Christmas Day, and evensong at around 6 p.m. on Christmas Eve. This is the one day, or in fact evening, of the year when we step inside the church, put aside our atheism for a moment and light a candle for our fellow villagers. Indonesians sing beautifully, and listening to the congregation singing 'Silent Night' during the candle-lighting ceremony can be a moving experience in any language.

The setting-off of fireworks has become a traditional part of the Christmas and New Year celebrations in the villages, and any guests staying at the lodge are invited to join us and the village children for a fireworks display after evensong. It is usually the case that some of the children can't make it through the whole church service, the anticipation of the fireworks to follow being too much for them. The latter part of the service is thus accompanied by rockets and so on being set off around the church by the children, which does nothing to improve the ambience or spirituality of the occasion.

After the service there is always tea and cakes outside the church, and it is after this that we take some of the village children back to the lodge to join our guests for soft drinks and fireworks, avoiding more public areas since the traditional palm roofs of the village houses are vulnerable to being set alight by stray rockets. The first time we did this we assembled the children on our back terrace, filled buckets with sand for the secure placement of the fireworks, bottles with water to form a safe launching pad for the rockets, and laid out the fireworks on our outdoor dining table, thus making things as safe as possible. We then made the mistake of leaving the little angels unattended for a couple of minutes, returning to find them in the midst of an Indonesian rendition of Armageddon. Roman candles were being held aloft or pointed in the general direction of the next child, rockets were being aimed into trees to add to their dramatic effect, and what was being done with the Catherine wheels does not bear the writing down. Intervention was pointless at this stage, and so we left them to their own devices until all of the fireworks had been very quickly used up. Nobody was hurt, and once the smoke had cleared we returned the dear children to their respective homes none the worse for the experience, and with foreknowledge of what to expect in subsequent years.

19

Natural Disasters

We are not here referring to ourselves, although certain of our friends and family members may feel the description apt, but rather we speak of matters geological and meteorological.

The North Sulawesi peninsula is moving at the rate of about 10 centimetres a year. It has recently (that is, over the last few million years) crashed into the southern part of the island, and is now heading out into the Sulawesi Sea in an anti-clockwise direction. This, at least in part, accounts for our living in a volcanically and seismically active area. Aside from the volcanoes themselves, there is a lot of thermodynamic action going on, which has resulted in areas with hot springs, warm, sulphurous lakes and hot mud. Our three most notorious local volcanoes are Klabat, which is the highest at just under 2,000 metres, Lokon, which is currently the most active and too dangerous to climb, and Mahawu, which is the easiest to visit and so the most visited.

I suppose it would be fair to say, if I may once again paraphrase, that to choose to make one's home near to one active volcano may be unfortunate, but to live so close to so many looks like carelessness, but you kind of get used to having them around.

There is a dirt road almost to the summit of Gunung Mahawu, which is usually open to vehicles, and from the clearing in the forest that serves as a car park it is only about a half-hour scramble to the rim of the crater. We include visits to Mahawu and the hot-spring areas in our tours of the Minahasa highlands, and are told by our guests that there are magnificent views from the summit, although we have never had the benefit of seeing them ourselves as whenever we have been there it has always been raining.

In places where hot-water springs occur there have been attempts to channel some of the water into spa-type baths, but none have been very successful as the locals don't bother with them and there are insufficient tourists around to make their maintenance worthwhile. For the same reasons, the paths through some of the hot-spring areas are poorly defined or not defined at all, and the unwary may accidentally step into hot, muddy pools, as has happened on more than one occasion to our dear guests. Fortunately there have been no instances of serious injury, and there is always plenty of hot water around to clean them up, the only lasting effect being the strong smell of sulphur that pervades the car on the journey home.

Earthquakes and earth tremors (we are not quite clear as to the difference, although we assume it is a matter of degree) are quite common, and we experience a few every year, varying in intensity from some that only a few people notice, to others that shake the house quite violently. Most memorable was one evening a few years ago when, as we were watching television upstairs, the room began swaying from side to side and anything not bolted down started moving about the room. The power failed and we decided it would be prudent to vacate the building. The rest of the village was also by this time out on the road. Once the quake was over, we checked each other's houses for damage as best we could in the dark, found that all was well, and after a reassuring cup of tea returned to our homes. That is to say, most of us returned to our homes, as this was shortly after the Aceh tsunami, and certain folk, fearing that a similar fate lay in store for Bahowo, loaded their worldly goods into wheelbarrows and anything else to hand, and headed for higher ground. We listened to the ocean (there was no moon so we couldn't see it) decided that it sounded okay and that such precautions were unnecessary. We went back to bed and slept soundly through the aftershocks.

The oddest thing about the event for us was that, with millions of tonnes of rock and earth moving around, we would have expected there to be some noise. In fact, apart from the noise of furniture and suchlike moving about, the whole event was completely silent. The water in our swimming pool had been sloshing about during the initial quake, and for an hour or so thereafter the surface of the water was moving, thus showing that the vibrations or reverberations went on after the quake was ostensibly over.

The morning after the Aceh tsunami itself, we woke to various emails and text messages asking if we were all right. We had not the least idea what had occurred, having at that time no satellite television or other direct means of obtaining news of the outside world, and thought that our friends had perhaps collectively become touchingly concerned for our general wellbeing. Some people thought that, since Aceh is in Indonesia and so are we, we must certainly be dead, and one friend phoned the Foreign Office and accidentally reported us missing. In fact there was not a ripple on the ocean around Bahowo, and certainly nothing more than usual. Indonesia is a very big place, and there is a lot of land and sea between us and Aceh.

Just as an aside, the then British Ambassador to Indonesia happened to be coming to the lodge for lunch on the day after the Aceh quake, being, as he was, on holiday with his family in Sulawesi at the time. Under the circumstances we didn't expect him to turn up, but in fact he came, and since at that time there were no reports of any British casualties, and he had sent a message of support to the Indonesian president, there was really nothing for him to do. Fair enough. We were at least able to confirm that we were alive and well, despite any reports to the contrary.

Earthquakes aside, though, we don't suffer greatly as a result of the local geological events. Our active volcanoes erupt in a minor way from time to time, which in fact pleases the local farmers as they gain from the covering of chemical-rich volcanic ash, and so crops improve that year. Lokon, as we mentioned before, is closed to visitors as it is sending out too much gas, and sometimes it sends out an ash cloud, which closes the airport for a short time.

More destructive, perhaps, are the mudslides and flash floods that can occur during the rainy season. The coastal villages are worst affected, particularly when there is a combination of heavy rain and high tide. The government has an ongoing programme to construct storm drains in the worst affected areas, but the low-lying villages are always vulnerable, and the road to Manado, which hugs the coast, is commonly closed to traffic. Despite being a coastal village Bahowo is fortunate in this respect, as most of the houses are at a generally elevated position above sea level, and it has quite steeply sloping topography. We also keep our storm drains well maintained, and the village never floods. About three years ago, one local village was completely washed into the sea after four days of torrential rain. The way the currents were running that day, the debris and flotsam ended up on the beaches of Manado Tua, one of the nearby Bunaken group of islands. This, very sadly, included the bodies of those who had fallen victim to this minor catastrophe. According to local information, one man survived the crossing, and one pig.

20

The Right-handed Bureaucrat

Normally with the bad parts of life there are compensating factors. (Clouds with silver linings, that kind of thing.) When dealing with Indonesian government offices, however, you have to look hard to find them. There is, perhaps and only, the sense of achievement gained when finally you have obtained your yearly work permits/immigration papers, or whatever elusive documents you are seeking at the time. If you will pardon the mixed metaphors, getting blood out of a stone is a piece of cake by comparison. What you do not have to look very hard for are the people in uniforms who haunt said government offices, as these have turned up in numbers at our front door, usually not leaving without at least the promise of future remuneration for services rendered, or to be rendered, be these real or imagined. We have earned our spurs somewhat now, have established our various contacts and 'friends', and so are not troubled so much these days. They are probably off haunting elsewhere.

We know perfectly well, of course, that we are living in somebody else's country, and are quite content to abide by the rules thereof and pay for the privilege. The question we frequently ask ourselves, however, is why the living here has to be so difficult. A process that could be completed in a couple of days or at most a week takes months, and if you want anything slightly out of the ordinary you had better bring sandwiches. In large part one can put this down to one of those 'cultural differences', which we will write about at various times and in various contexts during our narrative. As a general rule, Indonesians, and this includes Indonesian bureaucrats, have plenty of time. The people here regard 'Western' people in general as being 'stressed out' and always in a hurry. What to us is simple efficiency is regarded here as being an unnecessary rush. What difference, after all, does it make if documents are prepared today, next week, or in two months' time, provided that everything stays legal? They have a point, of course, but we are hard-wired into the idea that if something has to be done, it may as well be done as efficiently as possible. Get it done and move on, so to speak.

We, as foreigners, must carry plastic identity cards, which we apply and pay for in good time, but since these originate in Jakarta (that ultimate bureaucratic black hole where things go in but from which not even light can easily escape), invariably they take several months to arrive at our doorstep, and so for a good part of the year we are, strictly speaking, illegal. In reality we are very rarely asked to produce them, and if we do and they are out of date nobody seems concerned, since everybody knows how the system works, or doesn't work, depending on your point of view.

The key word of course here is patience, and in dealing with Indonesian officialdom and Indonesians in general one needs it by the truckload. The one golden rule of engagement at any level is: never become impatient and absolutely never lose your temper, as this is regarded as very bad form, and is always counterproductive. In the first place Indonesians have a very sensitive constitution, and do not respond well to being shouted at, and if you are less than cordial to government officials then your case will be buried even deeper under the mountain of paper. I think we are both moderately patient people; others we know or have known who are less so suffer as a consequence, and

118

don't make it for long in paradise. One must, in situations of extreme provocation, maintain a saintly and calm exterior, and then go outside and punch a tree.

In any case, we quickly learned that to pay somebody to undertake the various administrative processes for us is money well spent, and this we do; however, we are no strangers to the immigration offices in Manado, having spent several days there when we first arrived on these shores. It became very clear to us then that the connection in such offices between people being at work, getting paid for said work and actually doing the work are tenuous in the extreme. (They must just like wearing the uniforms.) In certain parts of Indonesia, notably Jakarta and Bali, there are agents who specialize in obtaining papers and documents for foreigners; however, there are insufficient expatriates living in the Manado area to justify anybody offering such a professional service. Being pioneers is, one supposes, always a mixed blessing. In our favour nowadays is that we have established good relations with a high-ranking official in a certain office who has rather taken us under her wing, and acts as coordinator between the various departments, understands the current system better than anyone we have previously encountered, and generally untangles the bureaucratic knots.

In general, though, during any meeting with government officials, pieces of paper are shuffled endlessly (it's the twilight zone again), there are always various different ways of achieving the same result, and you get the feeling that it is not so much that the right hand does not know what the left hand is doing (although this is perfectly true), it is rather a case that the right hand has yet to figure out what the right hand is doing. The money we hand over each year disappears somewhere into the system, and we never really know where it goes.

Things can, of course, be done in a perfectly legal manner through the back door, and we have found this to literally be true. A front-door entry entails the paying of administration fees to various 'desks' on the way up to the people who really matter, i.e. those who issue and rubber-stamp the documents. These people are best reached via a more devious route. Thus every year at a certain office, which had best remain nameless for purposes of this manuscript, a meeting is set up at an appointed time to bring one of our annual administrative processes to its spectacular and long-awaited climax, and we do not use the conventional means of entry into the building. Not for us the front door; instead, we are ushered in through the toilet. There is probably something metaphorical or deeply symbolic about this but one struggles to put one's finger on it. One just goes in through the toilet. We make our exit the same way with papers in hand, and try to avoid conjuring up possible mental associations between the two.

It is our hope that the day will dawn when documents and papers will be issued by helpful, smiling people, with some idea of the concept of public service, and that the system will be transparent, accessible and standardized, in place of the self-serving, mysterious and inefficient 'system' that has existed hitherto. We wish this not so much for ourselves, who are used to the system by now and have come to accept it as part of the whole deal, but for others that may come after, and most of all for Indonesia itself, which can never benefit in the long run and as a nation unless and until things improve. This day has yet to come; however, there are, it must be said, many reasons to be hopeful, and the system now bears no comparison with that which greeted us when we first arrived here. For instance, certain middle- and high-ranking officials and policemen have recently had their 'comeuppance' and been variously demoted, sacked, imprisoned or otherwise prosecuted for corrupt practices, and nearly all elections these days, be they local, regional or national, are fought on an 'anti-corruption' ticket. The current governor of North Sulawesi is doing sterling work in trying to clean things up, which of course cannot be done overnight for fear of throwing the proverbial baby out with the bathwater. So perhaps Indonesia has the bright new future that her people deserve, and dealings

Above: Views of Bahowo Lodge.

Above: The main road, Bahowo village.

Above: Raymon climbing a coconut tree.
Below: Village industry.

Above: The authors.
Below: View to the open sea from Bahowo beach, with fishing boats.

above: Staff meeting. Left to right: Raymon, Nyoman, Paula, Phil, Prama.
below: One of our local islands.

Above: The staff (with George).
Below: Mr Phillips, the village cowman, with Snowdrop and Babe.

Above: Bahowo football team, featuring Raymon (top right), Tom (bottom row second from left) and Nyoman (bottom row second from right).
Below: Queen Anne's Clinic.

Above: The staff. Top row left to right; Tom, Phil, Paula, Raymon, Prama, Nyoman, Melda, Sultje. Bottom row; Sebastian, Einstein (sons of Nyoman and Melda), and Kristy (daughter of Raymon).
Below: Village children, Bahowo.

with her government's servants will no longer put iron in the soul.

A matter of trust

If we may dwell for a moment longer on what are the very few negative aspects of life in Indonesia, then one of the most abiding of these would probably be the lack of trust that seems to be endemic here. Our own dealings with Indonesians are but an insignificant microcosm of a much wider phenomenon, and forgetting for now the difficulties that foreigners encounter here, it must be said that Indonesians treat each other no better in this regard.

If we may cite one example that may illustrate the point, it concerns a fairly well-to-do Indonesian lady who is a friend of a very good friend of ours. The lady in question was knocked over by a car and broke her leg rather badly. Being quite well off, she was able to pay for the services of one of the top surgeons in Manado to fix the problem, and he duly inserted three metal pins in her leg to reset her bone, and she paid accordingly. Again, because she was from the upper strata of society, she actually had private health insurance, which is a very rare thing indeed in Manado, and in order to receive recompense from her insurance company, she was quite reasonably asked to provide an X-ray of the leg, post surgery. On doing so she found that in fact only one pin had been inserted, instead of the three that she had paid for. Imagine if you will a well-paid, qualified surgeon who has an injured patient under general anaesthetic ripping that patient off. When asked what she would do about this, she said that she could do nothing, since she may well require the services of the same surgeon again to eventually remove the pin and, quite understandably, she did not want to upset him by bringing the misdemeanour into public view.

Unfortunately this phenomenon is not the preserve of any particular faction of Indonesian society, and even at village level, it seems, nobody can entirely trust anybody else. Everybody is looking for an 'angle', deals are done in an underhand way, and information has a monetary value in its own right. One of the teachers at our village school, who was responsible for paying the small monthly electricity bill for the school building, was recently found to be keeping the money, and the bill was not paid for several months. In this situation the school could well have found itself with no electricity. This kind of thing is sadly commonplace, and I suppose supports or reaffirms the time-honoured adage that one should not leave somebody who is hungry in charge of the biscuit tin.

At the lodge, it is sometimes the case that our guests do not pay for their accommodation until after they have left Indonesia and returned home, the agreement being that payment will be made later via bank transfer. It never occurs to us or them that the transaction will, for any reason, not go ahead. Between Indonesians, however well they may know each other, this kind of agreement would simply not happen.

Since friendship as we understand it is built upon absolute trust, and since, in our experience, this trust is a rare thing in Indonesia, then by definition so is friendship as we understand it.

21

Manado, a Tale of Two Cities

Manado is our provincial capital, a city of some 250,000 citizens, and it has changed almost beyond recognition since we first arrived in Sulawesi. The 'downtown' is still much the same, however. This is the original town centre, which is mostly run by the Chinese community, and consists of several hundred small shops, where you can buy everything you need and nothing that you want, from engine parts to plastic buckets. The central vegetable and fish market is also still situated here, and you can enjoy a very nice cup of tea for the equivalent of 6p, in one of the numerous local cafés. It has all the noise, bustle and chaos of any far-eastern town, although recently attempts have been made to 'clean up' and remove the illegal market stalls from the roadsides; this has resulted in the loss of some of its cultural charm but at least the traffic moves more freely. We find that some cities in this part of the world have become too 'sanitized' for our tastes, and it is good to know that at least in Manado it is still possible to mix in with the locals and see how they go about things, and their dealings with each other.

There was a need, however, to modernize the city, and introduce the idea of supermarkets, shopping malls and the like, and a huge amount of money has been invested, so far as we understand, from a central South East Asian fund, to finance the development of the city. The problem was that there was insufficient inner-city land available in order to do so. This was overcome by tipping several thousand tonnes of volcanic basalt into the ocean, and moving the coastline seaward by some 500 metres along a 5-kilometre stretch. This created enough new land to build several large shopping malls, a conference centre, supermarkets, cinemas, restaurants, night-clubs and many other amenities associated with a modern city. There have been the expected teething problems that go together with this kind of rapid development and attempted economic growth; for example, a couple of the biggest night-clubs quickly went out of business, and the largest of the malls closed before it was opened, presumably because the developer went bankrupt and nobody else had yet taken up the baton.

This process is still very much underway as we write this book, and it remains to be seen whether the huge investment will pay off for the city and people of Manado. We are neither of us macroeconomists, but it seems to be common sense that it will be impossible to sustain the required level of economic activity within the local community, and that therefore foreign visitors and Indonesians from other islands must be encour-aged to come to Manado and preferably invest money in the longer term by living and working in the city. In this respect, Indonesian bureaucracy and government are lagging well behind. In our opinion, if we may wax political for a moment, until Indonesia as a whole begins to open its doors to the 'big world' and make investment easier for foreign companies and citizens from richer countries, the long-term development of cities such as Manado will prove very difficult indeed. Currently it is possible to spend the whole day in town without seeing another foreign face.

In the meantime, those few of us who have established a

foothold can benefit from the newly available amenities, and the range of foodstuffs alone that it is possible to buy nowadays would only have been dreamed of two or three years ago. When we first lived here, there was no butter, cheese, olive oil, imported fruit etc. – now we can select from about six different types and makes of olive oil in any given supermarket, and the availability of a wider range of products has further and greatly improved the quality of our lives, and of course made it much easier to run the lodge, in the culinary sense. That staple of all Englishmen, Heinz Baked Beans, is now available in no less than three different types. Of course, we still have to make certain concessions to living in paradise, and soft mozzarella cheese remains an elusive commodity. Our friends and returning guests who are willing to give up luggage weight allowance to bring us foodstuffs necessary for the sustaining of life, such as decent cheese, were once given a substantial list of requirements. Nowadays the list is very much shorter, although Marmite remains an unattainable yet essential item, and the chocolate over here is largely of dubious quality.

The briefly aforementioned nightclubs fall into two distinct types. There are the small, rather 'seedy' clubs, which serve only beer, and where the musical selection is highly questionable. These are not (thank the lord) karaoke clubs as such, but visitors to the club are encouraged to take to the stage and sing, which the locals do with relish and foreigners do after imbibing a sufficient quantity of alcohol. Here all visitors are looked after individually by an Indonesian girl, her job being to serve beer, be a dancing partner and generally attend to her allotted guest throughout the evening. They will, if asked, provide other services, although neither we nor our friends and guests have ever made use of this facility. These types of clubs are hugely enjoyable, and we have passed many happy nights in such establishments.

To the other extreme are the large, modern, air-conditioned clubs, which offer a full, if still rather slow, bar service, live music by visiting bands, and a generally more 'Western' atmosphere. These are the preserve of middle- and upper-class sectors of society.

The rituals of dancing are also different in Indonesia to those that we are used to in England. Most noticeable is the fact that when dancing to 'disco' music everybody dances in lines; two lines, in fact, with dancing partners facing each other. To step outside these lines is to transgress the unwritten law, and it makes everybody else present feel uncomfortable. Perhaps they wonder whether two people dancing alone represents another line or potential line in its own right, and therefore question whether they should join it, or stay in the lines that they are presently in. During romantic songs, however, it is every couple for themselves, and they may take up random and non-static positions on the dance floor.

The other noticeable difference is that in England, and as far as we know everywhere in 'Western' nightclubs, it is usually the girls who dance first, with other girls; the classic 'dance around the handbags' situation. In Manado the girls initially take no part in the dancing, it is always the boys who dance first, in lines of course (no handbags), and with other boys as partners (it is quite acceptable and normal for boys to dance together). The girls at this stage of the evening sit around the perimeter of the dance floor watching proceedings, and will only dance when approached by a boy and invited to do so. Assuming that she accepts his invitation, she will be escorted onto the dance floor and escorted back when the dance is completed.

We hold parties at the lodge sometimes, when we or our guests are celebrating some event or other, which are held outside but under cover in our outdoor dining area. We have our own perfectly adequate sound system, with good sound quality, which we set up initially for the evening. However, if this is left unattended, as it almost always is, then our friends from the village will add speakers of their own by various dubious wiring techniques but without increasing the amplification, and the resultant sound is less than perfect. A compromise is always reached, and the parties are always good, and attended by people of all generations from the village. Here again we come upon one of our culture clashes, as the Indonesians, of course, always want to dance in lines, whereas the Europeans, Americans and so on find it hard to get the hang of this and tend to be random.

What is also noticeable to us about the nightlife in Manado is the fact that it is completely 'safe' and without any underlying tension or tendency towards violence. Fights are almost unheard of, and we have never witnessed any incidents of violence ourselves. Women and girls can walk alone in the streets of Manado at any time of day or night without fear, and in perfect safety, which is distinctly not the case in London and other cities that we know and love.

Driving in downtown Manado is an interesting business when one first attempts it, and some of our guests find the experience of being driven through town rather too exhilarating the first time that they undertake such a journey. The traffic moves in an organic, fluid kind of way, and the rules of the road are, shall we say, less well defined or apparent than in the West. It is perfectly acceptable to undertake a U- or three-point turn in the middle of a busy street, or to pull out of a side turning onto a main road with little or no regard to the oncoming traffic. Near head-on collisions are common when overtaking, as almost invariably something coming the other way is also overtaking. As with all systems, however, so long as everybody knows the code then it works perfectly well; we have never witnessed any incidence of 'road rage', and accidents are a very rare occurrence. Near misses, after all, are still misses. The drivers in general are courteous and polite, as befits the character of the people, and car horns are almost always used as a warning, as was their original intent, and rarely in anger.

About half of the vehicles to be found on the roads of Manado are private cars, almost all of them of the high wheelbase variety, the better to cope with the sometimes atrocious roads. Indeed, the last few years have seen an enormous increase in private car ownership, the number of car dealers growing roughly in tandem with credit companies that provide the loans with which the cars may be bought. The other half of the traffic consists of the small, always light blue minibuses or 'Microlites', which swarm the streets in their hundreds. These are privately owned, and the main form of public transport around the city and its environs. They are cheap, designed and licensed to carry up to ten passengers, and can be hailed at any point along their allotted route or hired privately by prior arrangement. The fact that they can be hailed anywhere, of course, means that they stop anywhere, usually in the middle of the road, and can really snarl things up with very little effort. They often have speaker systems installed that are massively disproportionate to the size of the vehicle, the noise emanating from which is deafening to passers-by and other vehicles. What it must be like inside defies imagination. Apparently the young people like to ride in such vehicles.

Even cheaper than the Microlites are the small, horse-drawn carriages called *bendis*, which carry two people over short distances around town. These have a certain traditional charm, and on one occasion our then twelve-year-old niece, Hattie (actually Juliet but we have never called her this), who is very fond of horses, asked if she could take a ride in one. We approached the *bendi* driver and asked for a ride. The conversation translated into English along the lines of the following:

'May our niece ride in your carriage?'
'Yes, where would she like to go?'
'Anywhere you like.'
(Pause for thought.)
'Okay, let's try again, where would she like to end up?'
'Here.'
(More pause for thought.)

'How far would she like to go before she ends up back where she started from?'

'Just around the block will be fine.'

She enjoyed the ride, the *bendi* driver was paid, and all concerned were happy, albeit that the *bendi* driver looked a little bewildered by the affair, and was perhaps left pondering whether there was money to be made by taking foreigners on pointless journeys.

Given the road conditions and amount of vehicles thereupon, the traffic moves around in a generally good-natured way. The minibus drivers can spend up to fourteen hours or more a day driving in cramped, hot conditions through crowded streets, for low wages, and even at the end of this ordeal will usually give a cheery smile and wave.

Incidentally, a further insight into the mindset of the Manado people may be gained when you pass a military HQ or army barracks in town, for written in large letters upon the walls of all such establishments are the words *Damai Itu Indah*, which means; 'Peace Is Beautiful'. Amen to that.

22

White Against Black

Another cultural aspect of the city of Manado is the large amount of chess played there, particularly in the downtown. Whenever we drive or walk through the backstreets, there are nearly always games of chess in progress, in the cafés, on the pavements, or wherever anybody has a chess set and anything that will serve as a couple of chairs and a table. The games will often draw small crowds, and I am sometimes tempted myself to pause awhile and check out the action. I have never yet done so, partly because when in Manado during the day we are usually intent upon doing what must be done and heading for home, and at night we are on our way to a bar, club or restaurant, almost always with guests or friends and in need of beer, and in any case Paula has no interest in the game.

In my early teens I was a keen player until, in common with most young men, my thoughts turned to other matters of a less cerebral nature. I continued playing occasionally into my early twenties, but thereafter and for the next twenty or so years I never so much as looked at a chess board. This was to change when we came to live here, as there are a couple of chess sets in the village, and on occasion our guests would bring travelling sets with them. Thus slowly my interest was rekindled, and eventually I found myself in town on my own and went in search of a set. The pieces I found were fine but the boards were not, so I asked one of our village carpenters, Nino, whether he could make a chessboard for me, to my specifications. He took on the job and a week or so later produced a superb board, the black squares of coconut wood, the white squares of chempaka, a light-coloured wood from which much of our furniture is made.

The set thus became an object of beauty in its own right, so now all I had to do was remember how to play. For those who do not play, playing chess is not like riding a bike – one may remember the moves, but putting these together in some coherent form is something else altogether. One has to relearn it. Thus on one of our visits back to England I asked for a couple of chess books for Christmas, and having brought these back with me I began the process of honing my chess brain, such as it is. Eventually I began playing again against Tom who, as I mentioned earlier, is a rather good player, and after a very shaky start my game has started to resemble somewhere approaching half decent. This is still work in process, but I have at least discovered the joy of the game once again, which has for me been another positive aspect of our move to Indonesia.

Chess, for those who have never played, and if I may be permitted to wax lyrical on the subject for a moment, is not like any other game. In the first place it is at once extremely simple and extremely complex. One can learn all of the possible moves and all of the rules of the game in an hour, and then spend the rest of one's life studying its complexities and subtleties. On one level it is two players moving thirty-two wooden pieces around sixty-four squares. On another it is about combat, strategy, attack, defence, deception, anticipation, and so on. On a still deeper level it becomes philosophical, although in a way that I don't fully get to grips with, and so have no chance of being able to write down. Someone far cleverer than I is needed to tackle that one.

The roots of the game go back thousands of years, and in a way it seems to me that each game that is played is part of an intellectual continuum, or a small part of an unwritten history. No two serious games of chess have ever been played the same, and each move by each player will change the rest of the game, in an almost infinite number of possible combinations. Every player will play according to his or her personality and, to bring the subject back to culture, there is a definite difference between the way the game is played in downtown Indonesia and how I first learned to play in England. Neither system is inherently better, but they are definitely different, so it could be said that, for example, Tom and I playing chess is a kind of small-scale and very specific cultural meeting.

It seems to me that chess in our native England has nowadays been eclipsed by modern pursuits such as computer games and so on, and if this is so then in my opinion at least, we are the poorer for it.

23

Language Barriers

We are neither of us natural linguists and have, after six years or so of living permanently in Indonesia, still gained only a fairly elementary knowledge of the language. We can understand most of what is being said to us, and make ourselves understood, but it does not flow easily off the tongue for either of us. Our linguistic inadequacies are constantly highlighted by our guests, particularly those from mainland Europe, most of who speak at least two languages fluently, and often three or four. This linguistic inadequacy must be a particular trait of native English speakers, or perhaps a reflection on the education systems of countries where English is the first language, since our American and Australian guests seem on the whole to share our mono-linguistic tendencies.

As we mentioned before, our staff could speak little or no English when we arrived in Bahowo, so we set about learning basic Indonesian, and teaching our staff English. It must be said that they have done rather better than us in meeting halfway, and around the lodge we tend to speak a kind of hybrid 'Englonesian'. We have invented new uses for words; for example, there now exists for us the verb 'to off', so we now 'off' the light switch. We would also 'very like a cup of tea', and so on.

In the Indonesian language there are no tenses, so we go to the market today, or we go to the market yesterday. There are also no genders, and the plural is achieved by doubling up on the object in question. For example, a child is an *anak*, and children are *anak anak*. The doubling of words also emphasizes their meaning; for example, *pagi* is morning, and *pagi pagi* is early morning. We have, for some reason, attained the habit at Bahowo Lodge of also doubling up on verbs. Thus we do not cut, we 'do the cutting-cutting', and we do not kill, we 'do the killing-killing' and so on. This, we think, is a peculiarity of the lodge.

Another 'problem big' when learning Indonesian is that there are several hundred different languages within Indonesia itself, and relatively small areas or groups of islands have developed entirely different language systems. For example, there are no less than eleven completely unrelated languages in the Minahasa region alone, which is an area probably about the size of Cornwall. So it is that the highland or Minahasa people cannot understand the coastal people, and vice versa. When our staff left their native island of Manado Tua to begin their secondary education in Manado, they had not the least idea what was being said to them. Manado Tua is about half an hour away by boat. It does seem incredible that such localized and isolated communities could develop over a long enough period of time to develop sophisticated languages, whilst having so little contact with each other that they do not share a common name for a tree.

There is now a standardized form of Indonesian taught in schools based on the Malay language, which is called 'Bahasa Indonesia', this now being the official language spoken on TV, written in newspapers and so on, and it is spoken widely throughout Indonesia, although by no means by everybody. Our staff have all learned to speak it, and so now speak their native 'Sangihe', as well as 'Bahasa', although amongst themselves Sangihe is still their natural language.

The matter is further complicated by the fact that Manado people speak a form of localized Bahasa known as 'Market

Manado'. This is generally what we use when speaking to our staff and other locals, but it would not be understood very far from Manado, and certainly not, for example, in Jakarta. Never go to Jakarta, by the way, unless need take you there. Aside from passing through the airport in transit, which we have had occasion to do a few times, I have visited the city itself only once, to see to some administrative matters, and that as far as I am concerned was once too often.

Much of the Indonesian language is quite poetic, or so it seems to us. *Mata Hari*, for example, translates as 'eye of the day', which is the sun, or sunshine. My personal favourite is the expression for sitting around doing not very much, just generally contemplating life: *Makan angin* or 'eat the wind'.

Finally on the subject of language, one of the first things one must do when moving to coastal North Sulawesi is to learn to say *'Wah!'* (cat) with suitable gusto. This is a general exclamation of surprise, shock or emphasis, as in *'Wah, srain* big!' (This translates into standard English as 'Oh my goodness, it is raining hard!') It is often kind of half whispered, and it takes a bit of practice to get it sounding right.

24

'Ello 'ello 'ello, what's goin' on 'ere then?'

In Manado and its environs, jobs are divided into two categories: 'wet' jobs and 'dry' jobs. A wet job is one in which it is possible to gain additional income over and above one's salary, and a dry job is one in which it is not. Being a policeman is definitely wet. It costs a lot of money, after all, to buy oneself into the police force, and one must get return on one's investment.

In the period building up to Christmas each year, roadblocks are set up around Manado, and cars are stopped at random to check whether there are certain items within the car. The certain item is different every year, one year it was a fire extinguisher, another year a first-aid box, still another year a red warning triangle, and so on. Of course, one is never told in advance which item is required in that particular year, and the standard on-the-spot 'fine' imposed for not having such an item is usually Rp 50,000 (about three pounds and fifty pence). The reader should bear in mind that this is about a day's salary for the average person in Manado, so this is lucrative business. Once word gets around, the shops quickly sell out of whichever item has suddenly become a vital part of motoring safety.

In the rare event of an accident, everybody, even if there is an aggrieved party, tries very hard not to bring said accident to the attention of the police. Car insurance exists here, in theory, but it is rather in the nature of virtual insurance, and serves absolutely no purpose in a real-life situation. So things are resolved there and then between parties, estimating the cost of repairs and spare parts, with some compensation for the wronged person.

We have had experience of this ourselves on one occasion, when, as we were proceeding through Manado in a privately hired Microlite, a vehicle shunted us from behind. This was clearly not the fault of Conny, the bus driver, and although there was no actual damage to the bus he was in negotiation with the other driver. All would have been well had not Conny, during the course of these negotiations, been knocked over by a motorbike. Now Conny, although not a tall man, is as hard as nails, and you have the feeling that it would take more than a mere motorbike to cause him undue consternation. He got up and dusted himself off, none the worse for the incident; meanwhile, the motorbike and rider had skidded off across the main road and were causing general mayhem amongst the oncoming traffic. This brought the event to the attention of a passing police vehicle, and half an hour of conversation ensued, during which it came to light that the motorbike rider was rather drunk. There are no drink-driving laws as such in Manado, and so long as you don't draw attention to yourself by flailing about in the road and bringing the traffic to a halt, then nothing is ever done. If you do flail about, however, then you are in trouble. The police thus had something to get their teeth into, and any money that would have come Conny's way went instead into the police benevolent fund. Conny drove us off feeling that he had not got the best out of the situation, as two avenues of possible financial gain had been closed to him.

In the villages, matters of discipline and disputes are usually resolved by the headman or elders of the village, police involvement being the last resort, and police are generally not welcome. This was demonstrated recently on one occasion when a disputed throw-in caused an altercation on the football field between two of the village boys. Their respective fathers joined in the fray, and a general free-for-all fight would have developed were it not for the fact that somehow (and nobody quite knows how) the police arrived on the scene. They were told in no uncertain terms that this was a village matter and that they should leave immediately, so that the fight could continue without further interruption until it reached its natural conclusion. The police, however, held a different view and took the four main protagonists off to the lock-up, where they were made to write 'I will not fight at football matches' one hundred times. This task undertaken to the satisfaction of the police, they were duly released with a warning.

Whole villages can, on occasion, become involved in organized fights, when all other means of settling differences have been exhausted. We know of one instance when two adjacent villages were in dispute over the right to mine gold in the region. The respective heads of village put forward their best ten fighters, and the villagers all turned out at the appointed time and place, whereupon at a given signal the fighters set about each other. These fights continue until one headman decides that his fighters have had enough, or are having the worst of things, at which point the fight is stopped, everybody shakes hands and the dispute is considered to be settled.

Some indication of the low levels of crime in Manado can be gleaned from the fact that the police do not work on Sundays. Nothing very serious happens around here, or nothing, at least, that cannot wait to be dealt with on Monday morning. Even then the police flag-raising ceremony can take up most of the morning, and on Fridays they have sports day.

The local police did have their work cut out recently, however, when Manado was host to the World Ocean Conference, and simultaneously to the Coral Triangle Initiative. Many important dignitaries, ambassadors, overseas presidents and so forth were in town for the occasion, and security and anti-terrorist measures were very much the order of the day. Police cars could be seen going up and down our local roads at great speed, or as great a speed as could be managed given the generally parlous state of said roads, the drivers apparently practising going really fast in case they were called upon to give high-speed pursuit to terrorists. We had a visitation from some of our local policemen, who were all for posting 24-hour security at Bahowo Lodge. Most of our guests at the time were nothing to do with the special events taking place, and although we did have a couple of minor delegates staying, we said that this would really not be necessary, but they could check on us every so often if they wished. Cassie and George, our two golden retrievers, like nothing better than to meet new people, and they came at the policemen with their usual canine enthusiasm, and with much wagging of tails. The policemen were terrified, being used only to the village dogs, which are very much smaller, and one of them climbed onto the dining room table. We put Cassie and George away, things settled down again, the policemen ate a mango to calm their nerves, and eventually left. We were left thinking that all a terrorist organization would have to do is turn up with a big dog and they could do more or less as they pleased, but perhaps that is disingenuous. Doubtless in the event of a genuine threat, the policemen would alight from whichever piece of furniture they happened to be on, and stand firm on behalf of the citizens of Manado.

As a final note regarding the police, we are fortunate at Bahowo Lodge in that Tom was formerly a policeman, before giving up his career to eventually work for us, and so he knows most of the Manado police, and some are his friends. During his time in the police force he presented us with a sticker to place on our car windscreen, which translated means 'Big Family Police'. These stickers are hard to come by, and impossible to obtain if one does not know a policeman or have friends in the police force. We are now ushered through roadblocks, this being one advantage of belonging as we apparently do, to one big, happy family.

If we may, we would now like to impart one small tale of village life, which is related to our current subject of the police.

The prisoner and the fish

Women in North Sulawesi society seem to enjoy a more or less 'equal' status to men. These are complex issues, of course, as anyone growing up in the West in the 1970s and 1980s will testify, and only the bravest of writers (especially boy writers – oops!) will tackle the subject head-on, without the usual plethora of provisos, disclaimers, exceptions and so forth. Indeed, introducing the very subject could be said to be questionable, and one might equally well say that men enjoy an equal status to women; however, as a means of further defining a society, and in the context of our story, I will plough on regardless.

If the number of women in management and government positions is a good bellwether as to the general state of things, then women are doing rather well, since a high percentage of the government officials that we encounter in our administrative lives are women. Many local villages have women as the village head, local and regional elections will always feature women candidates, and Mrs Megawati was, of course, president of Indonesia.

It is generally true here that girls do at least as well as boys at school, and the high number of girls who attain the all-important school certificate is in large part responsible for the number who go on to 'good jobs'.

Statistics can only go so far, however, and just as reliable is the 'feeling' that prevails about such matters. In the villages such as Bahowo, the general feeling is that women and men regard each other with equal respect.

Crimes of violence against women by men, including rape, are thought of as some of the worse of crimes, and can lead to severe punishment. Recently, a law was passed in Indonesia making

it 'illegal' for a man to attack his wife and not, perhaps signifi-
cantly, vice versa.

Thus it was that about one year ago Johnny the Builder Johnny
found himself incarcerated in the lock-up at our local police
station, having thrown a chair at his female cousin after a domestic
argument. The lock-up is a temporary holding place for offenders
before they go to trial and then perhaps to the main prison in
Manado. The room is bare, with no furniture and a barred door,
and nothing to do all day except ponder upon one's wrongdoing,
if indeed one is guilty thereof.

In any case, whilst there is no excuse for throwing a chair or
other item of household furniture at anybody, the crime was
clearly not premeditated, and Johnny the Builder Johnny is for
the most part a very mild-natured man, not at all given to throwing
things around in the general run of things. Nevertheless, he found
himself in the lock-up.

An Indonesian prison, incidentally, is not a place where one
should aim to spend any more time than one can possibly help.
I have been in one, as far as the visitors' room, when Mr Benjamin
the village head was incarcerated for a few weeks, as it happens
for hitting a woman who was setting about his children in a
violent manner. The family of the prisoner is expected to provide
supplementary food, and conditions are generally not good.

In the case of fairly minor offences such as chair-throwing,
where the injured party is not, in fact, injured, the offender has
twenty-one days to apologize before going before the 'Green
Table', where the judge will pronounce sentence. If the offender
thus apologizes, and the injured party accepts the apology, then
usually no more action is taken and the inmate is duly released.
Incidentally, in the case of Mr Benjamin, his wife was so aggrieved
at the way that her children were being set upon that she would
not allow him to apologize to the woman in question in time,
and so he served a longer than necessary sentence in the main
prison. One is made to wonder to what extent Mr Benjamin
shared her sentiments.

In any event, Johnny the Builder Johnny was still within his twenty-one-day limit when he turned up in Bahowo in a police car, escorted by what turned out to be two police warders. The villagers naturally thought that he was being released; however, it turned out that one of the said policemen was planning a fish supper and needed to buy a fish. Hearing that Johnny the Builder Johnny lived in a fishing village, he decided to take advantage of the fact and provided a police escort from the prison to Bahowo, where he duly purchased a fish and, having secured his supper, drove Johnny back to the lock-up.

In due course the necessary apology was forthcoming, all chair-throwing sins were forgiven and family relations have continued in a peaceful manner ever since, with both parties having perhaps gained somewhat more respect for each other. Such can be the way between men and women, equal or otherwise.

25

A Fisherman's Tale

Whilst on the subject of matters fishy, upon which we have touched in passing in previous chapters, it may be an opportune moment to devote some paragraphs to this most vital of local occupations. On most days, given fair weather and calm waters, the *londes*, or small, one-man fishing boats, leave the beach of Bahowo and set out, normally individually, in search of the day's catch. As the village is located within Bunaken National Marine Park, fishing in Bahowo is limited to line or spear fishing. Some fishermen are also particularly adept at catching fish by hand, a skill for which we have great admiration. It is as much as we can do to keep hold of a dead fish that has been delivered to the lodge, never mind keeping hold of one that is alive and trying to escape. During the tuna season, however, when the often huge schools of tuna can be seen disturbing the waters around the islands, sometimes accompanied by schools of hunting dolphins or pilot whales, the boats will work in unison, often at night, spreading nets between the boats. Tuna are deep-water fish, and so the boats can carry out this operation beyond the boundaries of the National Park, where net fishing is permitted, and at night at this time of year it is common from the balconies of Bahowo Lodge to see the horizon lit up with the hurricane lamps of the fishing boats. On occasion, if word has gone out to the village that we need fish, one of the villagers will arrive at the lodge with a wheelbarrow within which may be a tuna of 70 or 80 kilograms or more, large enough to provide our guests with delicious fish for several weeks.

Another, more intensive form of fishing carried out in the offshore waters of Sulawesi involves the use of what are locally known as *raks*. Picture, if you will, a very small house, not much bigger than a dog kennel, say one by one and a half metres, made of bamboo and palm leaves. In your mind's eye, place this house upon a flat raft made of bamboo poles, perhaps three by four metres in dimension. Such is a *rak*. These are floated out into deep water, and anchored to the ocean floor by means of a long chain. The onshore *raks* have closed nets attached below them, within which are placed young shoaling or reef fish, which the fisherman operating the *rak* will have caught, and which are sold to market once grown. Quite often these nets break before the fish reach saleable size, and the local sea is repopulated with young fish.

The deeper water, offshore *raks* are used for a different purpose. These can be located several kilometres from land, and from them, ropes are dropped into the water, and palm leaves and other large objects are tied to them. These act as lures and areas of shelter for shoaling, pelagic fishes, which are then trawled by the larger fishing boats from time to time. And there is a man who lives on the *rak*. He is dropped off at the beginning of the fishing season, and there he will stay for periods of up to three months at a time, his sole job being to radio the trawler when the fish are shoaling around his particular *rak*. Given that these *raks* are often in extremely remote locations, without sight of land or other *raks*, and the only time he will see another person is when a boat will call to supply provision for his survival, this must be an extremely tedious and lonely existence. His reward is a basic wage and a share of the catch.

Of course, shoals of fish will tend to attract larger predators, and occasionally a '*rak* man' will radio to shore in a state of terror, if a passing killer whale or other large beast should take a more than passing interest in his *rak*, and perhaps circle menacingly or take a tentative lunge at this foreign body in the water. There is nothing that anybody can do, of course, to ease his plight, save offer words of support or, more commonly, have a good laugh at his expense, since Indonesians like nothing better than to laugh at each other's minor misfortunes. Nobody to our knowledge has ever suffered injury as a result of such predatory attentions; it must just get boring out there.

Boredom, it seems, is not the only hazard with which our fishermen have to cope. Recently one of our village fisher friends, Rodlan, who is the eldest son of Aris and Sultje, had an encounter with a swordfish, in the course of which said fish speared him in the arm, after which its sword broke off. Rodlan thus returned to Bahowo with part of a swordfish stuck in him, and it required a two-hour operation to remove it. Fortunately his injuries healed quickly, and one hopes that the swordfish is not missing this part of itself overmuch.

26

Social Projects

In Indonesia, businesses such as ours pay income tax; individuals on the whole do not. At the village level, the people in any case earn insufficient money to warrant its collection. In the UK we were used to seeing half of our income disappear over the course of a year, and on the other hand we expected a health service, state-funded education, decent roads, and a public transport system and so on. Here there is insufficient revenue collected to properly fund such public services, and an insufficient amount of the revenue that is collected actually finds its way to the end product, such as new schools, road maintenance and hospitals.

Babies and children up to five years of age are well looked after in terms of inoculation against infectious diseases, and are checked over monthly. After five years, all free health care stops, and there is no free education. Families in Indonesia must therefore pay school fees from the day the child begins his or her education, to the day it ends, or until the money runs out, and premature termination of a child's education is common. Families must frequently make decisions as to whether they can afford treatment for sick relatives, and for how long the treatment can be sustained, since if the money stops coming, so does the treatment. Conversely, hospital administrators and doctors must decide whether or not a patient will receive health care on the basis of whether they think that said care can and will be paid for, as hospitals and surgeries can only keep going as long as they receive payment from their patients. Frequently a family is forced to make the decision to let an aged and sick parent die rather than render the whole family bankrupt, and this can and does cause enormous tension between brothers, sisters and so on.

Bahowo, of course, is no exception to these general rules, and it has been our great pleasure, over the years, to act as a conduit for money that guests and friends of Bahowo Lodge have donated to our village, which has, we know, greatly improved the lives of our fellow villagers in very many respects.

When we first came to live here, it quickly became clear that there were three major aspects of village life that were badly in need of improvement. These were transport, education and health.

In the first place there was no reliable bus service to and from the village. Perhaps the term 'bus' should first be defined, in case the reader has the mental image of the No. 26 turning up from time to time. Rural 'buses' here are converted pick-up trucks with a roof on, and can comfortably carry about ten people at a time. Uncomfortably they can carry fifteen or more people, and this is more commonly the case. In the city, the ubiquitous blue Microlites roam the streets in search of fares, and there are hundreds of them, but they rarely if ever come as far as the outlying villages. The 15 kilometres from Bahowo to Manado, for example, is well outside their range.

In the early days, the Bahowo Lodge jeeps were often called upon to take sick and injured people, or expectant mothers who had gone into premature labour, to hospital. There were cases where the person or child would certainly have died had we not been able to intervene, which was fine so long as our jeeps were available, but often they were out on tour, or in for repairs. The village needed its own bus, which would be permanently on standby for such times, quite apart from providing a regular service to and from Manado.

Such a service would mean that children could rely upon getting to the senior school, which is some 10 kilometres from the village, (the consequences of not doing so being fairly severe), that people could hold down regular jobs outside the village, and that goods such as coconuts and rice could be easily transported for sale at the main markets in Manado.

And so we embarked upon a fundraising venture, to raise money to buy the village a bus. In this regard we were very fortunate to know the then British Ambassador to Indonesia, who had a certain friend who was teaching at a school in England, and this school was looking for a project to support. This school is Queen Anne's School in Berkshire, England, and they have been wonderful in their support of our endeavours over the past few years. They hold annual fundraising events, the proceeds of which have come to Bahowo, and they have sent girls (for it is an all-girls' school) over to Bahowo to further cement relations between the school and Bahowo. With funds thus raised, together with money donated by many guests of Bahowo Lodge, we were able to buy and convert a bus. A certain Mr Reinier van Manen, whom we will mention later in connection with medical matters, and our friend the Baroness Fookes, were also in large part responsible for the setting up of the first bus to run from Bahowo.

As it transpired, raising the necessary funds and buying and converting our bus were not the end of our difficulties, as we then came up against the local transport police, who would need to issue us with a public transport licence. It has always been and still is our policy that all funds raised should be used directly for social projects, and as little as possible paid to government officials and others in 'administration' costs. We therefore had to tread a thin line between paying money from the fund, which would have got us the licence more quickly, and minimizing delays in having a working bus. In the end, we waited a little over a year for the licence, which in Indonesian terms is not a long time.

We decided to run the bus in the same way that the Microlites are run in Manado, insofar as we would charge a standard fee to the passengers, as set by the government. The difference would be that we would pay our driver a fixed wage as opposed to giving him a share of any profits, which is the normal way that things are done here. The bus would thus be more by way of a public service, rather than a profit-making enterprise.

When our bus began its daily rounds, our driver was subject to intimidation by other local bus drivers, who clearly resented our providing a competitive service to the one which they were not actually providing themselves, but eventually this situation was also resolved. This happened one day when two of the other Bangsuil brothers, Prama and Samuel (who are brothers of Raymon, Nyoman and Tom), approached one of the main protagonists in his bus, and asked whether he had objections to the Bahowo bus. We should explain that Prama is one of the leading gangsters in Manado, with something of a reputation for resolving disputes by non-verbal means. The bus driver began to protest, and meanwhile Samuel, who is very strong, picked up the rear end of the bus. The bus driver's protestations seemed to stop instantly and when asked again whether he had objections, he assured the brothers that he never really had any objections in the first place, and that it had all been a big misunderstanding. Since then the bus has been providing an invaluable service to Bahowo, making somewhere between six and ten trips a day to the outskirts of Manado, fully laden with goods and people, and Yohannis has a full-time job as our village bus driver.

Every Sunday morning he brings his account book to the lodge, together with any profit made from fares after the purchase of petrol and any servicing to the bus, we give him his wages for the week, and we 'park' the remainder of the money for future

154

servicing and administrative costs. In this way, the bus is just about self-financing. As a final gesture, and to add an English touch to the affair, we had a bus stop built in the village, complete with seats and a shelter. This now forms a meeting place and a focus for impromptu social gatherings in the village.

So, having dealt with the problem of transport, our fundraising efforts continued, and we were able to turn our attention to the village primary school. For our first project we constructed a hard-surface sports area for badminton, volleyball and football, and provided the school with the necessary sports equipment. The sports area being directly next to the sea, we erected high fences using timber posts and fishing nets, to avoid too many balls being lost to the ocean.

The village primary school has six year groups, from age five or six in year one, to eleven or twelve in year six, and on leaving the children attend the senior school in Manado or Tongkeina, a nearby and much larger village. The number of children in the classes ranges between two and ten children, depending on how productive the village women have been in any given year, and it is current government policy to issue two 'work books' for each class, one for the teacher and one to be shared between the children. This is clearly inadequate, so every year we buy enough work books so that each child has his or her own book in each subject, and we also provide pencils, paper and whatever other facilities are needed at the time. Last year we were able to buy and install two computers in the school, so that the children can learn basic computer skills.

Schooling in Indonesia is not compulsory, nor, as we have said before, is it free, and school fees, examination fees and uniforms must be paid for and bought by the parents or guardians of the children. Children are required to own four uniforms in order to attend our village primary school: red and white Monday to Wednesday, batik on Thursday, a shocking pink sports uniform on Friday, and brown and yellow on Saturday. Many families in Bahowo struggle to cover the cost of schooling, particularly as the children proceed through secondary school, so we started a sponsorship scheme whereby individual children are sponsored by our guests by a monthly standing order into our 'projects' account, which is held in the UK. At the time of writing we have twenty-five children under sponsorship, and are hoping to add to this number in due course.

The ultimate aim for any schoolchild, in terms of their educational aspirations, is to gain the all-important school certificate at the end of secondary school. This is an 'all or nothing' certificate, which is the only way forward to a career or further education. In the past, in Bahowo and villages like it, it has been the case that most people did not attain the certificate, schooling having been cut short out of financial necessity so that the children could start work, or because the families had been unable to fund their children, and it is our determined intent that all of the village children in Bahowo henceforth will finish their school education.

In Indonesia, schooling at all levels is very structured. There is a national curriculum, so throughout Indonesia every pupil will study the same subject at the same time, on the same day. The emphasis is very much on learning facts, numerical tables and so on by rote, with very little if any time set aside for creative thought, writing or art. Indonesians thus tend to be very good at, for example, mental arithmetic, and less good at thinking laterally or creatively.

Whereas in schools in the West classroom walls are often adorned with paintings and writings by the pupils, this is not the case here. Early on in our tenure, we decided that we would try to put this to rights, and so we bought paints and brushes and presented them to the teachers, thinking that perhaps half an hour could be set aside after school for some creative art work. The teachers thanked us accordingly; however, a few weeks later we noticed that no paintings had appeared. We asked the teachers if there was a problem, they thanked us again for the paints, but said that the problem was that they did not have any paper. We never again took anything for granted.

We are pleased to say that the Bahowo Primary school is nowadays cited as an example to other schools in the area and whereas before there was only one teacher for two year groups, we now have one teacher for each year group and a specialist sports teacher and English teacher. Since we have been able to buy the text books, equipment and so on, and the government pays the teachers' salaries, the families of the forty or so children who attend Bahowo School pay no school fees.

We have briefly mentioned Trefina and Ingrid as our first two graduates from Bahowo, and it is our sincere wish that we will be able to fund other willing and able students through college or university in the future. There are a few likely candidates in the village, who will be finishing school in one or two years' time, and we are monitoring their progress. One of the most important aspects of this for us is that the young people of the village understand that it is now possible for them to go on to further education, something that previously would not have been the case.

The other major problem that became very apparent when we first came to live in Bahowo was the total lack of any modern health care, apart from the monthly mother and baby clinic. The only time that any nurse or doctor would enter the village was for this specific purpose, and the clinic was held in the less than ideal conditions of somebody's front garden. There are healers in the village, and traditional, herbal medicines were, and still are, being administered; however, there was no access to modern medicines, bandages, antiseptics and so forth. So we set about the task of building a clinic in the village. Once again we are indebted to the students and teachers of Queen Anne's School for their part in raising the required money, and in honour of their efforts we eventually named the Bahowo clinic after their school. Thus it became 'Queen Anne's Clinic'.

The first stage of this process was to find and buy an area of suitable land for the building, and this was duly done after discussion with the village elders, the all-important land certificate being drawn up in the name of Nyoman. The clinic is in fact situated at the junction between the two village roads, in a very central position. We approached the local health authority and told them of our intentions to build a clinic, our condition being that we would provide the land, building and such medical equipment as was necessary and possible, and that the authority would provide all drugs and medicines, a nurse on at least a part-time basis, and regular surgeries by a doctor.

This was, after several meetings, agreed. The health authority was pressing us to hand over the land and building to local government control, but we insisted that we adhere to our conditions, so that the land and control of the use thereof would forever belong to the people of Bahowo, and to ensure that the building would be properly maintained. In the end all was agreed, and thus it was that a unique partnership was established between Bahowo village and the health authority.

And so the men of the village set about the task of building the clinic, for which we had provided a simple design, to include two rooms for surgery and a bedroom for overnight care, a bathroom, and a larger reception room in which mother and baby clinics and other village committee meetings could be held. We had established a system, during previous projects, whereby the village men would work for a 'social rate', which is somewhat below the normal day rate for builders, and some of those men unable to work full time on the project would give their labour free for one day a week.

Nothing happens here without great pomp and circumstance and, once the building work was successfully completed, the build-up to the official opening of the clinic began. This involved several meetings of doctors and officials in the new building, including a reception, with the required number of speeches, and with food provided by the women of the village. We only attended these as we felt necessary, and in general gave proceedings a wide berth until the day of the signing of the documents, which were to set out the agreements between Bahowo village and the authorities. This meeting was attended, as are most things of its kind, by the police, and on the way to this final meeting the head of the local police fell off his motorbike and so arrived pouring blood from various wounds. He could thus perhaps have become the first patient to be treated; unfortunately, though, the clinic was not yet set up to deal with the walking wounded, and the doctors didn't have anything with them, so we patched him up at the lodge and the business proceeded to its conclusion without further incident or injury.

At this meeting we raised the question once again of the nurse and doctor, and the health authority, in a rare moment of lateral thinking, proposed that if we were to build a house on the clinic land, then a full-time, on-site nurse would be allocated to Bahowo. All concerned agreed that this would be hugely beneficial, and well worth extra investment. A certain nurse called Martha happened to be present at the time, and she was told that she would be the nurse for Bahowo, and that she would come and live in the village. She looked somewhat bewildered by this turn of events, but said okay anyway, not in fact having been given much choice in the matter, and she has since settled happily into life in Bahowo.

We duly set about building her a house suitable for, as we thought, a single person living on their own. In the event she brought her husband, small child, mother and a 'baby sister', which in English parlance is a nanny. The building and house being eventually complete, we set about the business of providing equipment and medical supplies for the clinic. Some, such as bandages and cotton wool, we brought over from England during our subsequent trips there, others have been bought locally in Manado and, once again, the guests of Bahowo Lodge have been invaluable in their support. Most notable amongst these has been Mr Reinier, whom we have mentioned in connection with the village bus, who has been a regular visitor to Bahowo Lodge over the years, and has thus become our dear friend. He was instrumental (once again, sorry) in procuring, via the offices of a certain philanthropic organization in Holland, a great variety of medical instruments and equipment, from blood-pressure meters to a sterilizing unit, and so on.

So it is that Martha, our village nurse, now lives in Bahowo with her family, and daily provides first aid and medicines to the people of the village, and is always on hand to refer more seriously ill or injured people to the nearest hospital. We have regular surgeries by a local doctor, and the monthly 'mother and baby' clinic is now held in much more appropriate surroundings.

To close the story of our clinic, Martha is also a qualified midwife, and all village births are now carried out under controlled and safe conditions, under her tutelage. Previously, they would have happened in the village houses, under the watchful and no doubt competent eyes of the village women, who nonetheless lacked the medical training to sort things out if they went less than perfectly. The first baby born under Martha's supervision in the clinic was a girl, and in honour of her place of birth her parents called her, simply, Queen Anne. The second baby was also a girl, and so were the third and fourth. It was then supposed by everybody in Bahowo that, because the clinic was called 'Queen Anne's', that only girl babies could be born there. Thankfully the fifth baby was a boy, which lay to rest this superstition.

Other minor projects that we have been able to undertake include the building of refuse collection points in the village, repairs to the village road, the building of pillars at the entrance to the village and, of course, the purchase of the village cows. As an incidental footnote to bring this chapter to a happy conclusion, one of our cows has recently given birth to our first calf. We decided to streamline the naming process this time and avoid previous pitfalls by naming the calf ourselves. On the morning of the birth Paula happened to be in England, and I was reliably informed by one of the cow tenders that it was a boy cow. I contacted Paula by text asking her to provide a suitable name, which she duly did. A little later in the day I was told that the calf had in fact been diagnosed as being a girl cow (sometimes country ways can be mysterious), and so a few more texts later the first calf from the Bahowo herd finally bore the name Ermentrude. This will perhaps be appreciated by those old enough and fortunate enough to have been followers of the *Magic Roundabout*, which as I recall used to come on just before the 6 o'clock evening news.

We should emphasize again that, apart from the child that we ourselves sponsor, all of the projects that we have undertaken have been entirely as a result of the generosity of those who have donated money to the village fund, without whom none of this would have been possible.

We currently have an application pending for a certain sum of money from a central fund in Brussels, to construct and equip a specialist maternity unit as an annexe to Queen Anne's Clinic, and again our friend Reinier has been the instigator and go-between for this application. We may not be successful on this occasion, of course, as there are many worthy causes worldwide equally deserving and in need of support, but in any event we hope that by our efforts and those of everybody who supports us we will continue to bring improvements to the lives of the people of Bahowo, wherever and however we can.

If Indonesia is to prosper and find its way in the world in the future, then we believe that this will have to start from the bottom up, so to speak, in the villages such as Bahowo. If we continue to succeed in our quest to give the children here a good start to their education and, as far as possible, to look after their general wellbeing, then it will at least be one small step in the right direction. For the children and people of Bahowo who receive such invaluable support, whether individually or in general, from our friends and guests, it is a huge step. Our sincere thanks go out on behalf of all the people and children of Bahowo to everybody who has supported all of our village projects. As long as the support continues, we will do our part to improve the lot of the people in this small Indonesian village.

In our next chapter we would like to jump species and devote some pages to the creatures, wild and domestic, with which, at least for now, we share our planet.

27

Animal Magic

Domestic animals

Animals, of both the wild and domesticated variety, have played a major part in our lives in Indonesia. In the Christian villages, chickens and pigs roam free; in Muslim villages the pigs are absent, and are replaced by goats.

One of the things that we have had to adapt to is the fact that we are now much more up at the raw edge, as it were, of animal husbandry. Creatures here are put squealing into sacks and taken to market, and the fishermen would, and still do, bring all manner of just (or almost) dead creatures from the sea, which have to be weighed, wrapped, gutted and generally sorted before being served at table. This was all rather hard on the sensibilities of a couple of soft southerners, who had been confirmed vegetarians for twenty-five years or so prior thereto, and we have had to muscle up somewhat. I confess that on occasions when, for example, a bucket of live crabs has been presented to us, we have paid the supplier and put the crabs back in the sea. This has rather reinforced the villagers' belief that the silly English are sometimes prone to acts of insanity. One can see their point.

163

One incident that bought this into sharp focus was when one of our drivers took Alex, our eldest nephew, to buy a chicken for dinner. This was not a normal occurrence, as chickens are generally not a part of the daily diet of village people, but on this day we were to celebrate the anniversary of the founding of Bahowo. In any case, Alex, thinking that perhaps a trip to the local supermarket was in the offing, was most surprised when a very much alive chicken was purchased and placed on his lap on the way home, later to appear on the dining table. Whether he ate it or not has faded beyond memory, but he is also now a vegetarian, a fact upon which this incident may have had some bearing.

Anyway, as we were saying, the animals roam at will throughout the village. We are very much in favour of free-range animals; however, we have observed the perils of allowing pigs free rein. These creatures are no respecters of land or garden boundaries, and families of them often roam the grounds of Bahowo Lodge. This makes it difficult to establish many plants, especially anything herbaceous, and you may as well forget about growing vegetables. Woody stemmed plants are okay so long as you can get them established beyond the 'pig line', which is the highest point that a grazing pig can reach. We have high boundary walls that completely surround our gardens, but the entry gates are always a weak point. People leave them open, and even when closed the pigs are not deterred. We have tried various techniques to discourage entry, including wire mesh and barbed wire, but the pig is a very determined beast, and if they want to be somewhere they will bite, gnaw and generally worry anything that gets in their way. Oft times they will gain entry for the head region, and then get stuck halfway in. They haven't got the hang of reversing and cannot progress forward, and so get distressed and squeal as only a distressed pig can do. The only technique to be employed in these circumstances is to position oneself at the front end of the pig and give it a hefty kick on the snout. The pig will be shocked into RRM (rapid reverse movement) and walk away in as dignified a manner as possible under the circumstances, feeling somewhat disgruntled (with the emphasis on the 'grunt' perhaps) and rather put out but otherwise none the worse for the experience. I suppose that being stuck in this way is at least better than being stuck in the other sense in which the word is used in the context of pigs. Despite the best efforts of said invading pigs, Raymon has created for us a beautiful, lush, tropical garden.

Chickens are less of a problem in the garden, and tend to give good sport for Cassie and George, our golden retrievers. The chickens can fly passably well over here, especially if being hounded by large dogs, and can reach an altitude just above the boundary walls, thus making good their escape. They have little control over where they alight, however, and we have seen some messy landings.

We have met the village cows previously, and we have recently broken with Christian tradition by buying Einstein a pair of pet goats, whom he has named Bruce and Ruby. Einstein, incidentally, aside from being in our opinion the coolest kid in town, is the chicken king of Bahowo, the creatures having held a fascination for him since he was about five years old (he is now thirteen), and he usually has several on the go at any one time. These are to be seen variously roosting or scratching about in the garden of Nyoman and Melda, or wandering the village streets. Einstein comes with Nyoman to help out in the evenings at Bahowo Lodge serving at table, ostensibly to improve his English but we pay him pocket money for his trouble, and the money he earns pays for his chicken feed, or, if he is given a gratuity from a guest, he may invest in a new chicken. If we have no guests staying and he is made temporarily redundant, or he is unable to work because of school commitments, he occasionally gets into cash flow difficulties and has to liquidate some of his assets by selling a chicken, or applying to his mum for some temporary bail-out capital to see him though difficult times.

Most of the village houses have a dog in residence, mainly for security and pest control, so they are not 'pets' as we understand them, and they are largely left to fend for themselves. Cats are less common in the village, although they can sometimes be seen prowling the gardens at night. Most are only semi-domesticated, but they are not discouraged, as again they help to keep the rodent population down.

Cassie and George we bought as puppies from the only pet shop in Manado, which imports pedigree dogs for the rich local Indonesians and provides a full inoculation service. Most are small lapdogs, but occasionally they have larger dogs such as golden retrievers. Unfortunately, perhaps, many of the locals, who are not so familiar with dog breeds in general, cannot distinguish between the two at the puppy stage. On one occasion we took George in for one of a series of inoculations, and there happened to be a young couple who had just bought a very young golden retriever puppy. On seeing George they enquired as to his age. When we told them that George was four months old, they looked somewhat surprised at his size. Right on cue, Cassie jumped out of the car, thus giving a demonstration as to the size that a nearly fully grown example of the breed will reach. The look on the young couple's faces was a picture.

There is a well-established Kennel Club in Indonesia, and all dogs bought through their offices have pedigree certificates tracing their bloodline back several generations, and have the inside of their ears tattooed with a number for identification purposes. There is a policy of dispersing the dogs throughout Indonesia, to avoid problems of inbreeding with close relatives. Cassie came originally from Surabaya, and George is a city boy from Jakarta.

Before we leave the subject of domestic animals and move on to their wild cousins, we should just mention the local horse racing. Horses, as we have mentioned before, are used to pull the *bendis*, which are the traditional carts designed to carry passengers around the town centre, and are still a common sight in

Manado, competing for road space with the vehicular traffic. The big horses, however, are to be found in Tompasa, a small town in the highlands, where there is a long-established equestrian tradition. Virtually everybody in the town is in some way connected with horse racing, the smaller members of the community becoming jockeys, and otherwise stable hands, trainers etc. The racetrack itself, which is the only one remaining in the area, is a mile in circumference, and the horses are superb, many competing internationally.

Ownership of horses is, needless to say, a preserve of the rich of Manado, and race meetings, which are held every month, are a social event. Although we are not racing enthusiasts ourselves, we have been invited into the owners' enclosure a couple of times. The first time we went, we were unsure what one should wear to such occasions, and dressed in a way that would not look out of place at Epsom or Ascot. In fact, most of the local people, although smart, were not overdressed, and the trainers and owners all dressed as cowboys, complete with hat and boots, which, they proudly informed us, were imported from America. For the owners, a lot hangs on the results of races. Keeping and training a horse is an expensive business, and the prize money is very small. Therefore, the owners rely very much on 'form' and a horse with a good reputation as a winner can fetch good stud fees, and eventually be sold on for breeding, this being about the only legal way that the owners can recoup their investment.

Also sometimes featured at these meetings are cow races, in which each competitor drives a small chariot, pulled by a single cow. The cows, being generally less co-operative even than racehorses, take longer to line up at the start than does the race itself, which is apparently a thrilling and highly dangerous looking affair. I have never witnessed it myself, though Paula has, and enjoyed the spectacle.

Incidentally, gambling is illegal in Indonesia, and so does not go on at such race meetings, except illegally.

Wild animals

Snakes occur infrequently in our own lives, but they are generally very common hereabouts and found in great variety, and we
see a few every year. Recently, for example, we were clearing a
birds' nest out of the external electric meter box, and there found
a beautiful, striped snake curled up in the corner. We had to
disturb his slumber in order to remove the birds' nest, and he
glided serenely away into the roof rafters. He was somewhat over
a metre long. King cobras are quite frequently seen in the village,
and pythons come into the village at night and take the chickens.
Sulawesi is famous in snake circles for having some of the largest
snakes in the world, which are reticulated pythons; indeed, the
largest ever recorded snake was shot (unfortunately) here in 1912,
the beast being just short of 10 metres in length. They are found
sometimes by the villagers, curled up in the coconut and banana
plantations, although sadly we have only seen them for sale as
meat in the markets of Minahasa, and have not yet seen one in
the wild.

The birds that frequent our gardens are many and diverse. As
we mentioned previously, we are not bird experts ourselves, but
enjoy their company nonetheless. Kingfishers in various forms
and shades of dazzling blue are common, as they hunt in the
mangrove forests at the bottom of the garden, and quite often
we see eagles gliding along the shoreline. Our swimming pool is
dive-bombed by swifts in the late afternoons, in search of insects
or perhaps just having a drink, we are not sure which. Either
way they seem oblivious to bathers. We regularly have groups of
ornithologists staying at Bahowo Lodge, as many of the bird
species here are endemic, and it is, apparently, a birdwatcher's
paradise. Birds quite often enter the lodge and get into the guest
bedrooms, from where it is often tricky to remove them. They
tend to crash around into the windows until they get tired enough
to enable us to catch them. On one occasion a kingfisher got in
and our nephew Alex eventually caught it; the moment when he

stood holding a rather large kingfisher was a photo opportunity that got away. Bats often come in as well, by the way, but these are easier to remove as one merely has to open a door. They can't 'see' windows and so fly around in circles until they use echolocation to find the opened door and fly out, which is a far better system than the crashing about method employed by their avian counterparts.

A very high percentage of our local mammals, plants and reptiles are endemic to this area. In fact, it is true to say that Sulawesi is of great interest to naturalists in general. It was between Sulawesi and Borneo that Alfred Wallace drew his first famous imaginary line, noting the difference between species to the west and east of the line, and thus making suppositions about the origin not just of the species, but of the islands themselves. He spent much time in Sulawesi, which held a particular fascination for him, and, famously, it was shortly after leaving Manado that he wrote his all-important letter to Charles Darwin, expounding his theories on evolution. It was this letter that prompted Darwin finally to publish *The Origin of Species* and the world has never really been the same since.

We regularly organize day trips from Bahowo Lodge to the rainforests, the best locally being Tangkoko National Park. Here our guests almost always see tarsiers, which are amongst the smallest primates in the world, as well as black macaques, cuscus (a kind of tree-dwelling marsupial), our own endemic species of hornbill and others. Less frequently seen are deer and the North Sulawesi babirusa, or 'pig deer', also only found in Sulawesi, although these tend to be deeper in the forest and so to see them requires more time and determination.

28

Dive, Dive, Dive!

A large part of what drew us here to North Sulawesi, for our first holiday, was the possibility of diving and snorkelling the Bunaken National Marine Park, within the bounds of which Bahowo Lodge is now located, and although this was never intended to be a book about diving, we cannot let the subject go altogether without mention.

The park was set up to conserve the wonderful fringing coral reefs that surround the local group of islands – Bunaken, Siladen and Manado Tua – as well as the mainland coast.

The islands are all extinct volcanoes, with only Manado Tua ('Old Manado') retaining its classic volcano shape, the others having been eroded to within a few metres of sea level. All visitors pay an entrance fee to enter the park, the proceeds from which pay for administration and patrol boats. These are used to police fishing techniques within the park, and to ensure that the reefs and mangrove forests remain undamaged, as far as possible. Siladen is the smallest of the islands, and recently took it upon itself to claim some kind of quasi-independent status and charge people to moor boats, dive, snorkel or use the beaches or any other part of the island for any reason. The legality of this was always highly questionable, the islanders' response to any boat that refused to pay the tariff attempting to approach the island being to throw rocks at it, and those therein. At the time of writing, the main instigator of this system is on the run from the police, under charge of unlawfully obtaining money, and the beaches of Siladen are, we believe, once again open to all.

A percentage of the revenue from the park entrance fee is returned to the villages within the park, as compensation for loss of fishing rights, and the money is used for projects that will benefit the village as a whole, for example the installation of standpipes and header tanks, or drainage systems. Previously there was a total ban on all fishing within the park, but this proved to be unworkable since many villagers are totally reliant upon fishing for their livelihood. So limited fishing is now permitted using a line or spear gun, with a total ban on net fishing, bombing or the use of chemicals. The system is thus sustainable, and fish numbers are not depleted.

And so it is that the majority of the guests who stay at Bahowo Lodge come here to dive the magnificent coral walls and slopes within the park. In terms of our life, it was I who was the prime mover in respect of scuba diving, Paula never in fact taking to the sport with quite the same enthusiasm, so I hope that you will forgive my reverting to the first person singular for purposes of this more personal part of our narrative. My interest in scuba diving goes back to evenings spent as a young teenager watching the voyages of the *Calypso* on the television, and the fascinating underwater world brought into the living room by Jacques Cousteau, with his mesmerizing, heavily accented commentary. Last year we had the pleasure of having a certain Mr Bill Macdonald, an American film and documentary maker, stay with us at Bahowo Lodge. He was one of the original crew and cameramen on the *Calypso*, and gave us his personal insight into life aboard. He and his son Dustin, incidentally, had been commissioned to do research into the reefs of Halmahera, which is between Sulawesi and Papua New Guinea, but had been unceremoniously and prematurely asked to leave by the Indonesian authorities there, and so found themselves with time to spare and dive at Bunaken, but nowhere to stay. We offered them free accommodation under these circumstances, and as can often happen this worked greatly to our advantage, as in return they designed, photographed and produced a superb website for Bahowo Lodge, which we still use.

In any event, the voyages of *Calypso* had fired my young imagination, and I became determined that one day I would dive on a coral reef. Scuba diving was, at that time, nowhere near as generally accessible as a pastime as is the case nowadays, and was for years thereafter the preserve of the wealthy. My economic circumstances at the time rendered it out of the question for me, so my ambition would have to lay dormant for the time being, and it was not until many years later when we were on holiday in the Caribbean that I dived for the first time.

I well remember the circumstances; a local guy named Sly ran a two-tank operation out of a small hut on the beach near to our resort, and he offered to give me some basic training and dive with me. The training turned out to be very basic indeed, certainly compared to the sophisticated techniques used these days, but it was in this way that I took my first breath underwater. In fact, within five minutes or so of donning my buoyancy jacket and all of the initially bewildering array of pipes, fins, mask and so on that are the lot of the scuba diver, I was underwater and breathing independently of any recognizable air supply. Anybody who has scuba dived will know what a strange sensation this is the first time, and I cannot recall anything of that first dive, save only the freedom of movement I felt, which is impossible to experience in any other way, except, perhaps, in outer space. I was, in any event, hooked, and each morning that Sly was available during that holiday I would head for his hut and more of the same. Eventually I took the more conventional route to becoming a fully fledged scuba diver, finally taking my 'open water' qualification in the Cayman Islands and, a few hundred dives later, I have never really looked back to those first dives until writing these words.

Just by way of a conclusion to this personal aspect of my life, over recent years it has been my great joy and pleasure to accompany our two nephews, Alex and Edward, and our niece, Hattie (Juliet), on their first dives, by means and at an age not possible for me. The world is a very different place now, and the sub-aquatic world is no exception.

These days members of our species visit the great underwater in droves, and the world of coral reefs as well as most other aquatic environments, from the freezing sub-ice waters in the Antarctic to freshwater lakes the world over, have been opened to us. This has in certain respects been a positive development; witness, for example, the formation of Bunaken National Marine Park and the resultant conservation of the marine environment and the fishes that dwell therein. Of course, there is always a 'down side', and divers themselves will inevitably cause damage to the reefs, however unwittingly. Wherever humankind has adventured, from the time that our ancestors in Africa sharpened their first blades and used technology to improve their chances of survival, we have left our mark. Our return to the water, albeit by virtue of various artificial aids, after our distant relatives first flapped and crawled from the sea a few million years before, is no exception.

We have moved on a bit since then, of course. We now have a consciousness, we love, hate, worry and do damage. Technology has also developed somewhat from the sharpened stone flake, and to bring things right up to date, a factor that has worked in a negative way in my opinion has been the relatively recent easy availability of the underwater digital camera. I have in any event witnessed some disastrous diving techniques without this additional hazard, but its availability to and use by the average diver has led to some real damage being done, in search of the perfect photograph.

But let us not dwell overlong on the negative, for our visiting the reefs in ever larger numbers must also have increased our understanding and appreciation of this most delicate of ecosystems, and diving as a leisure activity has brought much joy and adventure to the lives of countless people, myself included.

In Bunaken, we are probably most famous for our magnificent wall dives, or 'drop-offs', since between the islands the sea plummets in places to over a kilometre deep, and the up-welling cool currents bring nutrient-rich waters to feed life at the surface. The temperature at the reef head stays at between 25 and 30 degrees Celsius, on a normal day the currents are mild, and the usually calm surface water conditions mean that we can dive all year round. Underwater visibility normally ranges between 10 and 30 metres, and the standard maximum dive depth is 25 to 30 metres, although the bottom of our local shipwreck is some 40 metres deep, and the maximum depth that I have ever dived here is 50 metres. The marine park is large enough, and the number of divers at any one time small enough, that almost always there is only one dive boat at any given site, so things never get crowded underwater, and the amount and diversity of coral and fish species is stunning. Just the fish species alone range from the 'small stuff', such as several species of ghost pipefish, scorpion fishes, butterfly fishes, angel fishes, frogfishes and seahorses (pygmy and otherwise), to the 'big stuff' such as barracuda, and reef sharks, a common sight here. Add to this list (which could have been much longer) the various types of dolphins, whales, sea snakes, turtles, starfish, octopus, nudibranchs, crabs, lobsters, eels and so on, and it makes for some very interesting diving at any level. After some ten years of diving here, I still see things that I have never seen before.

Perhaps just as famous in the scuba-diving fraternity are the world-renowned dive sites of Lembeh Strait, which are an easy day trip from Bahowo Lodge. Here one can engage in the rather unprepossessing sounding pursuit of 'muck diving', also know to divers as 'critter diving', since in, on and around the black sands of Lembeh live some of the most weird and wonderful creatures that one is likely to see anywhere, underwater or above.

Bunaken Park has also become famous after the 'discovery' here of the coelacanth, or 'fossil fish', which lives at great depths well beyond the reach of casual divers. This fish was first discovered off the coast of Africa, and was until then thought to have been extinct for millions of years. Then a few years ago it was noticed by an American marine biologist in a fish market in Manado. Locally it is known as *Ikan Raja*, or king fish, and the fishermen hereabouts have always know of its existence, although not of its biological importance. The fish is used to living at great depths and under great pressure, and cannot survive at shallower depths, and so nobody has managed to keep one alive in captivity.

Some years after this discovery, during our time here, an American-led diving expedition was organized at great expense to try to film the fish in its natural environment. For reasons unknown this expedition was supposed to be top secret, although everybody knew about it anyway. This took some weeks to set up, and during the preparation the local people would say 'They're looking in the wrong place.' The day of the first dive attempt came, and the local people said 'They're looking in the wrong place.' Unfortunately the fish was never found, eventually the expedition secretly left, and the local people said 'They looked in the wrong place.' In any event they couldn't see what all the fuss was about, as this most ancient of fish apparently doesn't taste very nice.

Special, secret expeditions to find old types of fish notwithstanding, scuba diving, if carried out using good quality, well-maintained equipment, and if all diving and safety codes are adhered to, is a perfectly safe pastime for the 'casual' diver. However, as with all activities, unfortunate events occur. This happened to friends of ours who were running a dive centre in the Manado area, when one day a particular guest had a massive heart attack 30 metres underwater. There is no way back from there, and there was nothing anybody could have done.

The deceased was brought to the surface and back to the dive centre, and placed, for ease of carriage, upon a trolley normally used for carting dive equipment. As it happened, there was a new intake of divers arriving at the time, and great pains had to be taken to keep the trolley out of sight of the new guests, by wheeling it from place to place, lest it create the wrong impression.

Of course the death of foreigners abroad causes certain complications, particularly in places such as darkest Indonesia. The next of kin must be informed, a post-mortem examination may be needed to ascertain the cause of death, and the body must be repatriated. It must therefore be kept in good condition. There are no available facilities in Manado for such an eventuality, and so the only course of action that our friends felt was open to them was to place the body in the freezer.

It so happened that the next day another body was washed up on the shore in the vicinity of the dive centre, and the local police were called. The body, which was of an Indonesian person, had no ID, and the police had no means of knowing from whence it had come. They called at the dive centre and asked our friends whether it would be possible to store the body temporarily in their freezer whilst enquiries were made, a request which they had to politely refuse, on the grounds that they already had a dead European gentleman therein.

What happened after that we never discovered, but in any event if you are considering taking up scuba diving, please don't be put off by this most unusual occurrence. I have now been diving for many years, and have never witnessed any serious illness or injury amongst my fellow divers. The underwater world must always be treated with respect, of course, and I have personally had a few brushes with anemones and soft corals, to which I seem to be particularly sensitive, and have some scars to prove it. As far as I am concerned it is a price well worth paying for the privilege of sharing, if only briefly, the underwater world with the wonderful creatures that dwell therein, and for fulfilling an ambition, or one might almost say realizing a dream, that began many years ago in a different life.

29

About the Lodge

And so, dear reader, by now we hope that we have provided some insight into the backdrop of our lives in Indonesia, and the means by which we got here. In this third and final part of our book, we will, if we may, attempt to convey as best we can how the world seems to us having done so. In other words, we will bring our narrative up to the present time.

Perhaps a good place to begin would be to deal with the business of our chosen profession of running a tourist lodge. We have explained, at least in broad terms, the roles of our various staff within our small business, for which, of course, we are ultimately responsible. What is more difficult to define is our position and function within it; in other words, what we spend our time doing. Having pondered this at some length, it seems to be the case that we can broadly divide this into three elements: practical, aesthetic and intellectual. If you will bear with us, we will attempt in this chapter to further define and analyze these three elements.

Before we do so, however, we may digress for a few moments to talk about how we work together. How is it possible for two people who have had such disparate and individual careers, not to mention personalities, to come together to form a tight, working unit? I hear you exclaim. Even if you have not exclaimed, I will take it upon myself to have a stab at answering the question in any case. In the first place, certain elements of both of our previous jobs are easily transposed across to the organization that is Bahowo Lodge, which, for purposes of the following explanation we will call 'the organization'.

For example, Paula has deep computer skills that I cannot begin to fathom, and so takes care of the IT side of things. She is far more numerate than I, so whilst I keep the daily accounts (I write things in a book) Paula does the tricky stuff on the computer at the month's end. She also has much better 'people skills' than I. This last is hardly surprising; after all, in my previous chosen career as a landscape gardener, it was often the case that I spoke to nobody and nothing throughout the whole working day except plants and building materials, which can hardly be said to be the same thing as talking to actual people since the conversation tended to be rather one-sided. On occasion I would come across another landscape gardener, but as a sub-species we tend rather to grunt at each other by way of passing the time of day, and bang rocks together for entertainment during tea breaks. When we opened the lodge, therefore, and I had once again to engage with normal human beings in a professional capacity, I had to learn the subtle art of conversation all over again. On the other hand I do have some design skills, which come in handy when designing extensions, outbuildings, gardens and furniture, and I am not afraid to mix it with the best of them when driving in Manado. I am probably good at other things, which escape me at the time of writing.

Anyway, to return to 'the organization', within this we have evolved a system whereby we have taken control of our own various departments. (Since there are only two of us, you may take it as read that we are heads of these, respectively.) For example, I am the transport department, responsible therefore for the safe and timely movement of guests and goods from point A to point B, as well as infrastructure and maintenance. Paula, for example, has household and catering (she is a wonderful cook in her own right), IT (as mentioned before), medical and statistics. I tend to answer emails (written communication department) and Paula is, as also mentioned above, better at guest relations (verbal communication department). Interdepartmental cooperation is of course common, which at certain times can take on a whole new meaning, if you understand me. Quite apart from the vital role of mutual emotional and other support, having two of us has meant that between us we cover most of the 'life skills' required to run the lodge. You wouldn't want to do this on your own, I would suggest. Anyway, let us return to those three elements that we spoke of previously.

Bahowo Lodge is a system, the constituent parts of which include the building, power and water supply, pumps, general infrastructure, vehicles, waste disposal system and, of course, people. Allowing for the necessity to buy in goods and spare parts, the system is almost self-contained; the only element that we mainly rely upon from the outside is an electricity supply.

The whole of this part of North Sulawesi receives its power from a hydroelectric power station, which is situated next to Lake Tondano in the Minahasa highlands. All is well so long as the lake has plenty of water, but when water levels drop, as happens sometimes during the dry season, there is insufficient water flowing through the power station, the electricity supply is rationed, and power cuts can be a frequent occurrence. These rarely last more than two hours, and are more of an inconvenience than anything more serious, and so we can ignore them unless they occur at a critical time of day, when, for example, our guests are showering having returned from their day's diving.

Just as an aside, our worst power cut ever lasted for three days, at the time of the unfortunate incident of Johnny Chainsaw and the coconut tree. After three days we and the village had had enough, and so on the third evening we took our vehicles and the Bahowo bus, and about twenty of the village men, and stormed the offices of the electricity company. The security guards ran away, and we confronted the officials, insisting that they tell us the whereabouts of the nearest technicians. Having located them, we hijacked them and their vehicle, a couple of Bahowo men riding shotgun within the front of their vehicle, with a couple more on the back, to ensure that they did not attempt any devious diversion, and brought them to Bahowo village. Here they worked long into the night, under the ever-watchful eyes of the villagers, until eventually our power supply was restored. We gave them a cup of tea for their efforts. Sometimes mob violence, or the threat thereof, is the only way to get things done.

This was, we are glad to say, a one-off incident. In the event of less extreme power cuts, we have a generator, for which we have built a concrete bunker somewhat away from the lodge. The bunker has been designed to minimize noise levels whilst allowing the escape of exhaust fumes. This is a delicate balance, which as it happens comes down in favour of the noise, and so turning the machine off (which is usually my job), involves entering a hot, incredibly noisy carbon-monoxide-rich environment, in which one could only survive for a few moments. Starting the machine is also something of a challenge; we have tried a battery and ignition key system, which never seems to work, and so we rely upon the services of Yohannis, our village bus driver, to get it going for us. It has a starter handle, which nobody has yet managed to use successfully, so Yohannis somehow hot wires it with a screwdriver, he being the only man who seems to be able to do this; yet another example of Indonesian practicality and pragmatism.

These are heavy machines, the bunker is located in a rather awkward position in a sloping area of the garden, and the initial installation needed about eight of us, using a system of running boards, wooden levers, and a great deal of physical effort before we managed to manoeuvre, push, pull and generally persuade it into its final resting place. The machine had other ideas, however, and tended to move about within the bunker when running, and risked doing itself physical injury, until, once again with some ingenuity, Yohannis and others lifted it onto some rubber tyres, since when it has been less active, stops trying to escape, and concentrates instead upon the job of providing the lodge with power in times of need.

Bahowo Lodge, in common with all systems, is liable to break down, and a part of our time is daily dedicated to ensuring that everything and everybody is working, as far as possible, to full capacity. In the practical sense this is our main function, since our staff are, at least theoretically, capable of running the lodge from day to day without us. In practice, however, the system will break down quickly without our control and intervention, and we must be around to ensure that everything is in place to provide service to our guests.

There is, we believe, an adage to the effect that whatever can go wrong, will go wrong, and usually at the worst possible time, and we have as far as possible to be ready for any worst-case scenario. The tendency towards pragmatism in the Indonesian mindset works against the concept of anticipation. In other words, an Indonesian will not deal with a problem until the problem is there to be dealt with. Foreseeing possible problems therefore falls into our camp, as well as preventing a 'problem small' from becoming a 'problem big'.

Everything in Indonesia works, after a fashion, and what goes wrong can always be fixed, eventually. The backup systems that exist in more technologically advanced societies, however, do not exist here. There are no 24-hour maintenance or emergency services, and no roadside recovery if our vehicles break down on tour. Thus if, for example, the water system develops a fault, then the system must be shut down until Mr Water can be summoned to the lodge, which will depend upon his mobile phone working (which is by no means guaranteed), his next availability, the availability of spare parts and so on, all of which means that it can be two days before he is here with everything that he needs to put things to rights.

Using a less dramatic scenario, our laundry service at the lodge is entirely dependent on there being dry, sunny weather. As there are no washing machines or tumble dryers our clothes-washer, Feni, does everything by hand, and dries the clothes on a washing line. As an aside, when we first came here, we made enquiries in electrical supply shops in Manado regarding the availability and price of washing machines and dishwashers. There were none, and nobody had so much as heard of a dishwasher, the idea of there being a mechanical device that washes dishes being a completely alien concept. Such a machine still does not exist in Manado, and one can quite see why such labour-saving devices are avoided. Why, after all, would one pay what to the average Indonesian is an enormous amount of money for a machine to do a job, when you can pay a human being who is quite capable of doing said job, who needs the work, and has plenty of time in which to do it. In any event, the power supply provided to the average Indonesian house would be inadequate to run anything like a dishwasher or washing machine. In the early days if we needed a new kettle we had to bring it from England or Singapore. Nowadays more powerful kettles are available locally, but the only time we bought one we plugged it in and then spent the next half hour or so pondering whether or not it was actually working. The water eventually warmed up a bit, but one would have had to plan a hot beverage a couple of hours in advance.

Aside from these purely practical matters, we concern ourselves with matters aesthetic (aesthetics department) and are constantly planning or implementing improvements to the lodge and gardens.

The lodge has been designed and built along very 'European' lines, having large rooms, straight lines, big windows, and so on, and all of our walls are painted white, inside and outside. The floors are tiled in various shades of white or light grey, with no patterns or other embellishment. This runs completely contrary to local design, Indonesians being lovers of bright colours and complicated patterns. Our furniture at the lodge has been for the most part handmade by local craftsmen, to our design. Thus for example we have bedheads with simple, sweeping curves, where an Indonesian would have complex, intricate carvings. Our dining tables and chairs, on the other hand, we prefer to be left rather 'rustic', and the locals would regard these as unfinished, preferring as they do a smooth, lacquered finish.

A small example of this cultural divide occurred on one occasion when we were buying some large ceramic urns for the lodge from the 'ceramic village'. These begin life, once fired, a subtle, terracotta colour. They are then invariably and very skilfully painted with Chinese scenes, flowers and so on, and some are decorated with very fetching waistcoats and bowties. We preferred them at the terracotta stage, and so ordered a batch to be fired with a clear finish. The craftsmen thought this a little strange, especially since we were prepared to pay the going rate for a painted urn, thus effectively paying them not to do something; nevertheless, they complied and the urns were duly delivered, unpainted. Having said that, the first one to be offloaded from the lorry was, in fact, a little ornate, and we thought that we may be in for an argument. It turned out, however, that this was an extra pot that they were giving us as a free gift, and all the rest were as ordered. We thanked them for the gift, and gave it away to one of our staff who would better appreciate its aesthetic value.

None of this is intended to imply that Indonesians do not make good furniture, for indeed they do, and on more than one occasion, as we have mentioned before, we have shipped containers of beautiful hardwood settles and chairs and very large ceramic pots back to England from Indonesia for our English homes. We have also bought a few fine pieces of furniture locally for the lodge, thus creating the contrast between modern European and traditional Indonesian, which works so long as you are careful.

The one place in particular where we are forced to make concessions to our Englishness is in the lodge gardens. Historically we have an interest in gardens and garden design, both professionally and in the making of our own, and so are used to the more subtle and subdued use of flower and foliage colour appropriate to the generally duller English light. Here in the intense tropical sunshine anything goes, really, and we tend to make everything as colourful as possible, mixing and blending colours that would be unthinkable in the typical English garden. In our opinion at least, it looks fantastic.

The third, entirely different aspect of our work could be said to be, at least in the broad sense, intellectual. This occurs at the interface with our guests, who are on holiday, with everything that implies and requires. We are in a sense the buffer, or at least the go-between, 'twixt our guests and Indonesia, and one of our functions is to soften this potentially massive cultural divide. We have lived here for six years or so, and are just starting to get the hang of it; to do so in a couple of weeks would be asking too much. That said, living as we do in a small fishing village, our guests will often *jalan-jalan* (walk about) in the village, where they will always receive a warm welcome from the people, and we regard the accessibility to this aspect of the 'real Indonesia' that we offer as being an integral part of our guests' stay at Bahowo Lodge.

We usually eat with our guests in the evenings. Every year we have several large groups staying, of perhaps fifteen or twenty people, and these groups are often more self-sufficient and insular. They are usually part of a dive club, so are here ostensibly to scuba dive every day, and their holiday revolves around this activity. Our job then becomes more a matter of logistics, in terms of transport, meals and so on, and our main point of contact tends to be with the group leader. The majority of our guests, however, are people travelling alone, in couples or smaller groups. We always give people the option of eating alone, but have found that the general way of things is that our guests prefer to have their evening meal around a shared table with their fellow guests, in which case we often join them. In this way the interaction between our guests, and us and our guests, becomes more personal, and conversation over the evening meal becomes a focal point in the day. Indeed, at certain times of the year, it is rather like hosting dinner parties every night for several weeks, which is one of the most enjoyable aspects of our working life.

We have all the raw materials here for creating wonderful holidays; warm seas, deserted sandy beaches, coral reefs, rainforests, mountains, local culture, superb Indonesian food and so on. Our job is to make all of this available and accessible to people, whilst ensuring their comfort and insulating them somewhat from the raw edges of Indonesian life.

These people, our guests, come from anywhere and everywhere in the world, and therefore are themselves from very diverse cultural and social backgrounds. A person from northern Europe is essentially different from someone from southern Europe, who is different again from somebody from India, America, Australia, Africa or from wherever they may wend. Within our native northern Europe, English people are different in essence from Dutch people, who are different again from German people, and so on, and the fact that we are all now 'Europeans' has, we are glad to say, done nothing to change this fact. Bringing people together who can share their very differing take on the business of life can be immensely rewarding work, and we would personally have it no other way.

And then, of course, within these broad national divides, everybody brings their own persona and agenda to bear on the situation, and may be here to relax, seek adventure, find their private space, party, discover Indonesia, not discover Indonesia, and any combination thereof.

The overriding factor with our work is the great pleasure that it has been for us to meet and spend time with the many guests who pass through our doors. We have made many lifelong friends over the years, met fascinating, stimulating people, and it is our abiding pleasure that a high percentage of our guests return, be it every few years, yearly or several times a year, as is sometimes the case.

Of course there is always a down side and we also on occasion get to meet people who are a problem walking about on two legs, and there is nothing you can do with or for them. We have a short-list of about six people who would not be welcome if they attempted to return to the lodge, and a couple of borderline cases. Six in as many years isn't bad. Our philosophy has always been to try to create a 'homely', informal atmosphere at Bahowo Lodge, and we have found that in general people have responded warmly to this, and we have some great times.

As with all systems that involve people, there is always the element of human error, and since at least most of the time we think of ourselves as belonging to this species, we are not immune from its vagaries.

For example, there was one occasion when a new group of guests had just arrived, and I (for it was only I) became convinced that one of them was following me around. Wherever I was, there he would be, and he seemed to be moving from room to room with almost supernatural speed. It was not until later that day when I encountered him twice in the same room that I realized that there were in fact two of him, and that 'he' was identical twins.

And then there was the case of the three guests – one woman, two men – who, unusually, spoke very little English. The woman and one of the men shared the same surname, and since they had booked one double and one single room, we showed them into a double room, with which they seemed satisfied, and the single man into a single room. The single man became most distressed, he kept saying 'This is no my room', 'Yes, this your room', 'This is no my room' and so it went until finally he could take no more and said, with some passion 'I want to sleep with my wife'. Not an unreasonable standpoint, and it was then that we realized that it was he who was married to the lady, and that the two with the same surname whom we were attempting to persuade into another room were in fact brother and sister.

We are required by law to register all of our guests with the regional police department, and so ask all of our guests to fill in registration forms when they check in at the lodge. In the box marked 'Profession' these same three guests had written 'Evangelist'. We naturally made the assumption, therefore, that they were deeply religious people, and that they were no doubt high in the church hierarchy in their own country. Certain aspects of their behaviour did not really bear this out; for example, one of them smoked heavily, and they did not seem to have a generally very godly countenance. Nevertheless, each one of them wore a cross around their neck, and we became convinced that we were correct when, on the first Sunday of their stay, they told us that they were not going to scuba dive on that day. Thinking that this would transgress some deeply held religious conviction, we thought this quite natural, and asked them whether they would like to attend service at the village church. They looked a little unsure, and we thought perhaps that they felt that attending a church of a different denomination would be inappropriate; however, they agreed to go, and were duly marched off to morning service by our staff. The next weekend we assured them that the same arrangements had been made for them, and in fact they were in residence for three weeks, and so attended church each Sunday.

It was not until the last day of their stay that we broached the subject of their faith. It turned out that none of them actually believed in God, but felt that they had to put something in the 'Religion' box. One of the men was a carpenter and the other was a train driver. (There is, by the way, no Religion box.) The dawn can come anytime, even when the sun is about to set.

The lodge has seven guest rooms, consisting of five double or twin-bedded rooms, including a deluxe room, a suite of two rooms and a family room. Our normal maximum capacity is 18 guests, although arrangements can be made, by strategic placement of additional beds, for twenty or more people. There are occasions every year where demand outstrips supply, and we vacate our own bedroom to create the additional required sleeping space, and at such times in the past we have taken ourselves off at night to a mattress on the lounge floor. This system worked well, and was of only minor inconvenience to us. However, even this was sometimes not enough, and guests who have changed their plans at the last moment and decided to extend their stay with us have also elected to sleep on the lounge floor. On one such occasion we were in the habit of watching movies in bed before lights out, which made certain other guests rather envious, and so they also would vacate their room and bring their mattress into the lounge. We have since extended the lodge, giving ourselves more living space, and are glad to say that we have slept alone ever since.

On the whole, though, technical breakdown, human error and occasional over-capacity notwithstanding, matters roll along in a fairly orderly fashion, thanks to the always well-meaning efforts of our staff, and we like to believe that we offer a unique holiday experience to our guests, from wherever they may come. Going to church on Sundays is no longer compulsory.

30

Ethical Issues

One cannot undertake a venture such as that which has become Bahowo Lodge without thinking long and hard about matters of ethics. For us this has been for the most part done retrospectively, since, in truth, when we first began our venture we probably gave little thought to the matter. So once again, our proverbial horse may have bolted, but better late than never, I suppose, and so we attempt in this chapter to have a stab at tackling the subject, thorny though it may be.

When we lived in England we did not regard ourselves as being particularly 'rich'; in an Indonesian fishing village, however, we are rich beyond local comprehension, in the same way as we ourselves could scarcely comprehend the idea of being multi-millionaires. We have, despite our early problems, made a good life for ourselves, and our moving here has improved the quality of our own lives to a great extent, and this has been done by using our relative wealth to employ the labours of people far poorer than ourselves.

Conversely, we have, over the past years, passed such money as we have earned by our business endeavours exclusively into the local economy of Bahowo and beyond. By this means we have seen a marked 'improvement' in the villagers' standard of living, not just in more general and 'social' terms of the clinic, bus, school, and so on, but also in terms of the individual people that we employ and from whom we buy goods. When we first arrived here in Bahowo there were perhaps two television sets in the village, around which the villagers would gather to watch football games and so forth. Now it is the case that most of the village houses have televisions, and Johnny the Builder Johnny even has a satellite dish in his front garden. This phenomenon is not, of course, entirely due to our being here, but the lodge has without doubt created an economic dynamic in the village.

Insofar as this may be seen as progress, things have got better for the village by our being here, and it appears, at least on the face of it, and at least financially, to be a win-win situation.

There is, however, more to it all than money, and this was brought into focus for us recently on a trip we made to the other side of the peninsula. Despite our best intentions, we had never been beyond the highlands and down to the south coast of the North Sulawesi peninsula, and so we decided to make the trip. The journey takes only some four hours from Bahowo, the roads being reasonable by local standards as far as the descent from the highlands. From here the road becomes little more than a dirt track, and although we eventually came within view of the ocean, we put in some hard miles through beautiful forest before we eventually reached the coast. Here we drove into a small fishing village that is about as close to an image of paradise as it gets. Traditional houses were set along a sandy beach, with swaying palm trees and gently lapping water. Beautiful children greeted us, and we were made welcome in a very Indonesian way; chairs and a small table were placed in a shady part of the beach, and we were served with delicious local coffee. We swam for an hour or so in the crystal clear waters, before we had to retrace our steps back to the uplands. We were apparently the first white people ever to enter the village.

The point of this is that, during our short time there, the villagers were asking Raymon, who was driving that day, what they had to do to encourage more foreigners into the village. Should they make a place especially to serve coffee? What would we like? They told Raymon, and he later told us, how expensive (or in fact how cheap), it would be for us to buy land on the beach. Would we perhaps like to build a small guesthouse? As I write this I have tears in my eyes, not for the first time whilst writing this narrative. In the first place there are echoes here of Bahowo before our arrival, but a large part of you wants to just tell them to stay as they are, progress is not always progress, and not always good in any event. They live a simple life in a beautiful place, which many of us would envy.

But of course this is not really the point, and this is only a romanticized outsider's perspective. Their lives are hard; they fish, they farm coconuts, they grow rice, and they survive. They have no appreciation (how could they?) of the beauty of their surroundings, since they know no others.

And another part of you wants to help them. To build another lodge, to bring in foreign money so that they too can have some of that which we take for granted. And so would come the televisions, and eventually the satellite dish, and why not? It is within our power or the power of others like us, to give them what they clearly want, and we cannot sit in judgment as to who should have what, who should 'progress' and who should not. We could help them, as we have helped the people of Bahowo, to take a small step closer to those things that we are, in a way, trying to get away from.

Of course, we cannot resolve this critical debate. As with so many such dilemmas it is possible to put forward good arguments on both sides, and humankind has ever invaded his fellow man, with good or evil intent, for any one of many reasons, and the resultant changes brought about have seldom if ever been entirely good, or entirely bad. Thus have we ever moved forward.

It is possible to travel in a matter of hours from such a village to the massive, bright, shining metropolis that is Singapore, and which may as well be on a different planet, and to put one of these village people who live such simple lives into one of the seemingly endless shopping malls would be like putting a man on Mars. To them, perhaps, this would be a vision of paradise, whilst to others it is the very vision of hell. After all, the journey from the beaches along which we first colonized our planet to the bright city lights has taken our species several million years, and one could argue that we would perhaps have been better staying where we were.

In any event, if we decide to consider such matters, we must be careful how we tread, however good we perceive our hearts to be, for there is no truer saying than this; that the road to hell is paved with good intentions.

31

And in the End

And so, dear reader, we come to the end of our tale, at least insofar as it can be written down in these pages. When I sat down on the first morning clutching a hangover and strong coffee, and wrote the word 'Foreword', I had little notion of where the book would take us, other than having a few mixed-up notions, stories and subjects in my head, and indeed I wondered then whether there was a book there at all. In the event, the tale has grown in the telling, so to speak, and in the writing of this book it has seemed to us that there are many subjects that we could expand upon, and we could in truth have written a longer book, but for now at least we will be content, lest the book get away from itself.

In the writing of our story we have had to pull some punches concerning some aspects, opinions and ideas in order not to offend the sensibilities of certain individuals or the citizens of Indonesia in general, and in order to safeguard our own position in our adopted country. We have nevertheless, we believe, given as open and honest account as we could. Further expansion of certain matters would require a more clandestine medium or circumstance for open discussion (or 'open speak', as we say over here), such as over a few cold beers on a warm tropical evening.

Anyway, we thank you for bearing with us, and hope that you

will have found at least some parts of this short history interesting and perhaps enlightening, and leave with some sort of impression as to how our lives have been and are still in this most wonderful, beautiful, and sometimes mad country. Here time has an elastic quality, the truth is not always quite the truth, and a lie is not always quite a lie. Behind the maintenance of sanity here there lies the prerequisite to think well outside the box; indeed, in truth we probably threw the box away a long time ago.

And so what do we make of it all? The question is rhetorical of course, and however we may consider that which we have done, we have made our mark, for better or worse. If there is some grand conclusion, or overriding or underpinning philosophy such as we touched upon in our introductory paragraphs, then it will perhaps have to wait until another book, at another time, if such is ever written. Perhaps things only ever become clear in retrospect, and whatever else our story may be, it is surely unfinished.

For us, for now, it is enough that we have taken ourselves away and apart from our own kind, I suppose in a way to see if the proverbial grass is really greener on the other side. And for us the gamble has paid off, regardless of our difficulties in the beginning and what may happen hereafter, and in many ways this is a better place for us to live, not least because we no longer say goodbye to each other on a Monday morning and meet again on Friday evening, as was often the case when we were pursuing our former lives in England. Back then our careers had developed to the point where our work took us apart from each other for a good part of the working week, and we would in a sense live our lives for the weekends.

From where we stand now, if ever we were to ask ourselves whether we would do it all over again, the answer must be: absolutely. If asked whether we would recommend that others do the same, the answer would be: absolutely not. We have seen relationships fall apart and projects and endeavours fail here, not for want of effort or good intent, but perhaps it was just the wrong idea at the wrong time for the wrong people.

There is a hotel some miles along the coast from Bahowo Lodge, in an even more isolated location than ours, with, as far as we can see, no village nearby. The hotel is quite large and grand, having I would say well over 100 rooms. It is located on a small peninsular, with sandy beaches on both sides, it has a fully stocked shop and dive centre, and even a large, plastic Christmas tree in the foyer. There is a newly laid tarmac road leading up to its front entrance, which means, one assumes, that the right people were paid the correct amount of money. Under a glass case in the reception area is a scale model showing the rest of the proposed development, with, amongst other things, retirement homes and a golf course, the whole being called 'Paradise Village'. The entire place is completely empty and falling rapidly into disrepair. We came upon the hotel quite by chance some three years ago, having moored our boat at the end of the long, timber jetty, which was at the time still serviceable but becoming dangerous. Curiosity got the better of us (well, it would, would it not?) and we walked into and around the hotel for an hour or so. The swimming pools were cracked and empty, what had once been landscaped gardens were overgrown and dilapidated, and the building itself was, in our opinion, beyond repair or renovation. The Christmas tree is always in the foyer.

We know of another large hotel in Manado, which was built, equipped and ready to open, with food in the kitchen and staff standing by to receive its first guests. On the day of opening the authorities moved in and prevented trading as the hotel did not possess some vital piece of paper or licence, and it was some two years before the hotel was able to open its doors. Perhaps the 'Paradise Village' hotel suffered a similar fate, or perhaps the money ran out, or the guests didn't come. In any event a large amount of money and endeavour was wasted, and these are not isolated cases hereabouts.

Even if any given venture is commercially successful, of course, to seek perfection or perpetual happiness in things material or circumstantial is to chase after a phantom. We have briefly met people since living here who have for many years been travelling the world in search of their own nirvana, their own perfect place, which we strongly suspect does not exist. In order to live somewhere with a contented soul, you have to arrive with one, and what does seem clear is that wherever we go and however much we change our circumstances, we take our essential selves with us. In the end we are who we are, wherever we are.

In any case, our small story will go on. Indonesia has pushed us to the edge and pulled us back again, and brought into sharp focus parts of ourselves and each other that perhaps we never knew existed. How long we will stay here in Bahowo is, of course, something we cannot yet tell. Perhaps the epicentre of the next earthquake will be under the dining room floor, or one of our volcanoes will end its long life in a final, massive explosion, and take all that we have built down with it. Or perhaps the Indonesian government will not wish us to live here anymore, for we are guests in this place, strangers in a strange land, and will ever thus remain.

Whether we could ever happily live in England again is something that we ask ourselves from time to time. After all we are English, and in some odd way we feel more English living here than we do when we return sometimes to our native country, and there are times when the different comforts of our old life seem very appealing. Everywhere looks better from a distance, in time as well as space.

For now, at least, Sulawesi continues to work its magic on us, and as long as it does then we will stay, and Bahowo Lodge will continue to do its work. What will happen after our inevitable and eventual departure, whether this be by accident or design, is something that we cannot foresee. It would perhaps be fitting if the lodge were to be left empty for nature to go about her business, and for the jungle to be allowed to unmake that which we have made. In the end nothing is ours, even that which we call so.

For the moment, though, we are here, and the tropical rain, the clear blue water, and the beautiful sunrises and sunsets have become a part of our daily lives. All of these things, and of course the people who have made this home for us, have all worked their way deeply into our souls, and insofar as one can understand or define spirituality, this place has it by the bucketful. And we are of course fortunate to have been able to make the choices that we have, and to be able to continue to do so. We may all be on the road to nowhere, but some of us are lucky enough to be able to decide how we get there.

I suppose one could conclude by saying that we have, by making this potentially cataclysmic change in our lives, for whatever reason, put ourselves and our love on the line, and all have been found equal to the challenge and have probably been made the stronger for it. If the last ten years have been nothing else, then they have been an adventure, and as a friend said recently, if life is not an adventure, then it is nothing.

We could undo everything we have built, or just walk away, move back or move on, because wherever we take ourselves we take our love, and in the end, it's all about love.

THE END (of the beginning)